CHASING
IMMORTALITY

CHASING IMMORTALITY

MANCHESTER CITY'S ULTIMATE SEASON

STEVE MINGLE

First published by Pitch Publishing, 2023

Pitch Publishing
9 Donnington Park,
85 Birdham Road,
Chichester,
West Sussex,
PO20 7AJ
www.pitchpublishing.co.uk
info@pitchpublishing.co.uk

ISBN 978 1 80150 657 1

Typesetting and origination by Pitch Publishing
Printed and bound in Great Britain by TJ Books, Padstow

Contents

Introduction

'I SWEAR you'll never see anything like this ever again!' And ten years after Martin Tyler delivered the most memorable commentary line of the Premier League era, City did their level best to prove him wrong. Trailing Aston Villa 2-0 with a quarter of an hour to go, in a match they had to win to take the title, they scored three goals in five minutes to turn the game on its head and break the hearts of Liverpool fans. Again.

When you win the Premier League it's a great season whatever else happens. When you win the league four times in five years you're a great side. Definitively. And yet as the celebrations at the Etihad got under way, there remained a sense of what might have been. That hideous night at the Bernabéu, in complete control only for two goals in a minute from absolutely nowhere to deny us a place in the final, still hasn't been erased. I swear you'll never see anything like that again either. Bloody well hope not anyway.

For many outside the club, and most inside it, winning the Champions League has become an obsession. Pep insists that the important thing is to reach the final stages, to consistently 'be there' and one year your number will come up, the fine margins will fall in your favour. But there's this nagging, infuriating niggle that we can't put that argument to bed. The argument that you're not in the elite until you've won the Champions League. So we'll enjoy the summer, but not as much as we might have done.

Since that dramatic May day, there have been some significant departures from the squad. The loss of Fernandinho, a club legend but now edging past his prime, has long been anticipated, but the exits of Raheem Sterling, Gabriel Jesus and Oleksandr Zinchenko are a little more surprising, especially as, unusually, they've all moved to potential rivals for silverware. We've lost plenty of stellar performers over recent years – Vincent Kompany, David Silva, Sergio Agüero – and coped well enough, but four senior players in one hit is a lot. Equally, Pep's always recognised the need to refresh the squad every year no matter how successful the side has been. Fresh faces, hungry for success that they haven't previously experienced, bring a new energy as well as enhancing competition for places.

So who will come in to fill the void? We'll belatedly welcome Julián Álvarez, frequently touted as the new Sergio Agüero, who it's confirmed will stay at City for the new season rather than remaining out on loan with River Plate. A new second keeper, Stefan Ortega, arrives from Arminia Bielefield. And Kalvin Phillips, impressive for both Leeds and England, comes in to replace Fernandinho. It's hard to see Phillips being anything but an understudy to Rodri, allowing the increasingly influential holding midfielder to have a rest when fixture congestion kicks in, but we shall see. Pep has always been full of surprises.

But the headline signing, the one that's whetted appetites not just among City fans, is Erling Haaland. It's the first time we've taken on a ready-made superstar. Well, apart from Robinho, whose elite status proved to be merely in his own mind. No one expects Haaland to fall into the same bracket. His goalscoring record speaks for itself, but it's a while since we've played with an out-and-out striker and a crucial factor in defining our season will be how quickly we can adapt to him and he can adapt to us.

The overwhelming majority of observers expect that Haaland will prove to be a huge success. But will he? His acquisition will require a serious change in the team's style of play. The fluidity and midfield superiority afforded by the use of the false/occasional/no nine will be replaced by a bloke who by all accounts scores tons of goals but doesn't do much else. His record thus far is phenomenal and, although the Austrian and German leagues might not be quite such difficult places to rack up the goals as The Greatest League In The World ™, his record in the Champions League and international football is equally spectacular. It's going to be a fascinating tactical challenge for Pep, but fascinating tactical challenges are what keep him alive.

If Haaland will be under pressure to deliver the goods, then so will last season's marquee signing. Acquired from Villa for a monstrous £100m, Jack Grealish's first season had been seriously underwhelming. And there were plenty of told-you-so merchants out there, at a loss to understand not just how Grealish would fit into our style of play, but also how what on the surface appeared to be an 'all about me' persona would go down in a dressing room where humility and team ethic were everything. As the weeks went by he consistently struggled to impose himself on games, and in the matches that really mattered he spent most of his time on the bench.

It's not as if he's unpopular with the fans, although I suspect there's a strong correlation with age, with the youngsters loving his social media-friendly personality and folks of my generation thinking that any bloke who wears an Alice band might as well wander round with a neon sign saying 'I'm a twat' strapped to his chest. The simplistic conclusion many of us came to was that it suited him better to be the big fish in a small pool, the undisputed star of the show. That's never going to happen at City, where everyone's a star but no one's *the* star.

When I first saw Kevin De Bruyne at City I was stunned by how much he reminded me of Colin Bell. Not just in the way that he played, his dynamism and energy, but the way he moved, his gait. On numerous occasions he's done something which has instantly transported me back 50 years from the pristine grass of the Etihad to the mudbath of Maine Road.

As soon as I saw Grealish, he similarly put me in mind of Rodney Marsh, that almost lazy way he drags the ball along, teasing defenders, slowing things down. Undeniably supremely skilful, but not necessarily to the benefit of the team. Many of us struggled to understand what we wanted with a player who slows the game down and takes lots of touches. Pep explained that someone who slowed the game down and took lots of touches was *exactly* what he wanted, drawing opponents in before releasing the ball to areas where we could more easily make progress. But it just wasn't happening, or at least not very often, with Grealish repeatedly, timidly, simply playing the ball back or, when he attempted something more ambitious, finding his attempted cross or shot blocked. More than anything he was just so predictable, so easy to neutralise, and his lack of impact was reflected in the seasonal statistics, with a meagre three goals and three assists. City had no fewer than ten players with more direct goal involvements than Jack. Stats tell only a fraction of the whole story, but here they were consistent with the evidence of our own eyes. Still, many have been the players who've taken a season to adapt to playing in a Pep team, and the manager himself had repeatedly pronounced himself happy with the player's contribution. But for sure the pressure was on.

As for the rest of the squad, well, what's not to love? Ederson as good as it gets in terms of what Pep demands from a keeper, Walker with pace undimmed and improving on the ball year by year, Dias a rock since the day he arrived, Laporte, Stones and Aké proven defensive allies and Cancelo as creative and inventive an alleged full-back as they come. Rodri's developed into the league's best holding midfielder and further forward, the many and varied talents of Bernardo, Gundo, Phil, Riyad and Kev, all of whom had made huge contributions to our recent successes, could be mixed and matched to suit the circumstances and tactical approach required. Contrary to popular myth, the squad of senior players isn't huge, but with so many of them having the versatility to play in more than one position, Pep still has plenty of choice when it comes to selecting his teams. And it means that he doesn't have to leave too many players out in the cold.

It will be the strangest of seasons, with a six-week interruption to accommodate the World Cup. But, as ever in the Guardiola era, City are pre-season favourites for the title, with Liverpool almost universally expected to be our most dangerous rivals. They're a formidable opponent and the battles between us have developed into one of the great rivalries, if not yet in terms of longevity then certainly in terms of quality. On only eight occasions have teams amassed 92 points or more in a 38-game season, and City and Liverpool are responsible for six of them, twice both hitting the mark in the same season. The bar has been raised in terms of what it takes to win the title, which means that even at the start of the season there's little margin for error.

7 August, 2022, Premier League: West Ham 0 City 2

'He would have punched his team-mates in the face'

BEFORE THE new campaign starts in earnest, City and Liverpool lock horns in the Community Shield. Liverpool, so close to completing the quadruple last season, had to settle for the two domestic cups, winning them both without scoring a goal in either final. But theirs is the name on the FA Cup and with both sides having been active in the transfer market, the build-up to the game is befitting of a far more meaningful occasion. While City have acquired Haaland, Liverpool now boast Darwin Núñez, signed from Benfica for £85m. On the face of it this dwarfs Haaland's fee, but the slug of money City needed to pay his agent to get the deal done brings the numbers much closer. Not to mention the sizeable disparity in wages. So which of them will get off to the better start?

Our recent performances in the Community Shield have generally been underwhelming, especially in the Pep era. We've often put out understrength sides, with the manager insisting on giving players a minimum period of complete rest before they return to training. Equally, there's no doubt that Pep does ascribe some importance to this match as, on the last occasion we won it, he was quick to claim it as a 'proper' trophy. I wish he hadn't. As far as I can recall, José Mourinho was the first to do this, desperate as he was and remains to bolster his tally of silverware in support of his claims to be classed as one of the greats, rather than yesterday's man, a has-been who elite clubs no longer want anything to do with. Pep really doesn't need to sink to that level.

City field a very strong side, although their surprising shortage of pre-season friendlies means that they're seriously undercooked. Liverpool have managed to fit in a few more warm-up games and it shows, as they look the sharper team from the outset and take a deserved lead through Trent's deflected long-range shot. He celebrates with that horrible finger to the lips hushing gesture to City fans, as though the goal really matters. City almost respond before half-time, with Haaland twice getting a sniff of goal but unable to take advantage.

In the second half, Julián Álvarez forces home a scrappy equaliser and the game is evenly balanced until Liverpool bring on Núñez with about half an hour to go. He puts in a high-energy cameo and is a proper handful for the tiring City defenders, first winning a penalty when his header is blocked by Dias and VAR deems it to have been a handball – there'll be plenty more where that came from this season – before he then heads home to put the game out of our reach. There's still time to claim a consolation, and when Adrián parries a shot into Haaland's path, the striker has the perfect chance to open his City account. However, from just six yards out, he balloons the ball over the crossbar to wild cheers of derision from the Liverpool fans. Haaland reacts with a wry smile, as if to say, 'Don't worry, I'll be having the last word over you guys', but for now he just has to suck it up – not just as the bones are picked out of the match by the pundits but also over the next week, as the social media trolls go into overdrive.

When the final whistle blows, the reaction of the Liverpool players is quite extraordinary, and their fans follow suit. I can scarcely believe my eyes. It's as if they'd won the Champions League. Maybe it's a release of the frustration left over from the end of last season, when the two big prizes eluded them at the last. The cliche of the day will be that 'they've put down a marker' for the season to come. For City, their fans and especially Erling Haaland, it's a season that can hardly come quickly enough. The Sky Sports feed claims that Liverpool had claimed the early bragging rights – well, no one likes to brag more than Liverpool fans – as though anyone is going to remember this game for more than a week, the time it will take for the Premier League to get under way.

At least there's an element of perspective from some of the pundits, with Jamie Carragher lamenting that 'the Haaland banter compilations will be everywhere this week, just like Núñez last week [after he missed a couple of sitters in a friendly, for God's sake]. From muppets who've never kicked a ball in their lives,' while Roy Keane, after observing quite rightly that Liverpool were the better team, said, 'But there is a week to go yet. City looked slow out of the blocks last year but it's about how you finish, and City are good at that.' And no one knows that more than Liverpool, making it all the more surprising that they should respond to their win in such excessive fashion. Or maybe they already had a sense that this would be as good as their season would get.

So after having to endure a week of intense social-media mockery, Haaland lined up at the London Stadium with something to prove. Another week of training left City in far better shape as they dominated from the outset without quite being able to make the breakthrough. Then ten minutes before half-time, Gündoğan slid a clever ball through to Haaland, allowing him to demonstrate one of his great assets. His acceleration over ten yards deceived Areola, who'd slid to smother the ball but instead took out the striker as he nicked it around him. It was an obvious penalty, and Haaland grabbed the ball in a manner which brooked no argument from any of his colleagues. Having taken the time to compose himself, he sprinted forward and side-footed his shot all along the ground, a couple of inches inside Areola's right-hand post. He sat cross-legged in his celebrated 'Zen' pose before receiving the congratulations of all his team-mates.

It was a clinical, confidently dispatched spot-kick but it was the striker's demeanour prior to its execution which really impressed his manager. 'The way he took the ball to take the penalty, I said, "Oh I like it!" I think if one of his team-mates were to take this ball, he would have punched him in the face. That is a good sign. You've got to be self-confident, ambitious and have a ruthless mentality.'

Midway through the second half comes the moment City fans have been waiting for. As De Bruyne receives the ball from Rodri, Haaland makes a run and Kev's pass is weighted perfectly. No one has a chance to get even close to catching him. All he has to do is slide the ball past Areola, but it's the way he chooses to do it which is both fascinating and impressive. As he approaches the ball it would be natural to take another touch to set himself up, but he instead alters his path to run outside the ball, allowing him to open up his body and strike for goal with his first touch. Areola is beaten easily as Haaland runs on to receive the adulation from exultant City fans. It's a master craftsman's finish – where most would have taken two touches, Haaland took care to ensure he needed only one, minimising the scope for something to go wrong. It will soon become apparent that this is what he does. 'The ball was in the back of the net before you could say "most devastating partnership in European football",' observed Matt Dickinson in *The Times*.

If the goal demonstrated an obvious way in which City could utilise Haaland's qualities, it equally sent a crystal-clear signal to future opponents on what they had to do to combat them. With De Bruyne's capacity for delivering incisive through balls allied to the striker's unnatural speed and composure in front of goal, only the bravest or most foolhardy would attempt to defend with a high line. Even those who normally did so would surely adapt their tactics when facing City.

Afterwards, David Moyes said that his team's struggles had been less about Haaland and more to do with João Cancelo and Kyle Walker pushing into midfield, forcing his wider players to come inside only to then see City quickly spread the play out to Foden and Grealish. 'They changed from last year. We did really well against them last year. Walker and Cancelo played either side of Rodri, they played with no full-backs. We hadn't prepped for that because we hadn't really seen it.' And Grealish, although his performance hadn't been spectacular, was name-checked by Pep afterwards for his part in the second goal, taking the ball in the left-back position and sucking opponents in, 'The goal belongs to Jack, keep the ball, attract opponents, slide a ball to Rodri.' In other words, exactly what he'd been bought to do.

For now though, it was all about Haaland, who if nothing else had banished the reaction to the previous week's mishap to the archives of oblivion. Instead, he was met with a welter of compliments and predictions about how he was about to take the Premier League by storm. Alan Shearer predicted a 40-goal haul, Roy Keane between 30 and 40, Paul Merson a more modest 25.

Guardiola was pleased with the big improvement from the Liverpool game and summed up the witless knee-jerk reactions of pundits, reporters and social media misfits perfectly. 'One week ago Erling could not adapt to the Premier League, now he's alongside Thierry Henry, Alan Shearer and Cristiano Ronaldo.' But he was already on to a theme which would be returned to almost *ad nauseam* throughout the season, 'We would like to add something to his game to be a little better ... not just a guy who scores goals.'

But just a guy who scores goals will do perfectly well for now.

2

27 August, 2022, Premier League: City 4 Crystal Palace 2

'These games are why I'm here – to turn things around when there are difficult times'

CITY'S FIRST home game was as eagerly awaited as any in living memory. Everything already seemed to be centring around Haaland and you couldn't help but wonder what effect this would have on him – and on his team-mates, most of whom were used to getting plenty of column inches themselves rather than being relegated to the supporting cast.

The opponents were Scott Parker's Bournemouth and City produced an accomplished and dominant display to brush them aside. Haaland showed a different facet of his game to set up the opener, holding up the ball on the edge of the area and, despite a stumble, prodding the ball through for İlkay Gündoğan to fire confidently home. Bournemouth had shown little attacking ambition and when they finally made a meaningful foray downfield, they were made to pay for turning over possession. A quick pass from Foden fed De

Bruyne, who ran directly at defenders reluctant to commit themselves, before bending an exquisite outside-of-the-foot shot into the far corner. Watching the goal again, you can see how two defenders were preoccupied with Haaland, whose run dragged them away from the more immediate danger. It would be the first of many 'invisible assists' for our new striker.

De Bruyne then turned provider, a sweet pass being controlled perfectly by Foden, who squeezed a shot through the keeper's arms to put the game completely out of Bournemouth's reach and allow City to move into game management and energy-conservation mode in the second half. Just one more goal was added – Jefferson Lerma turning João Cancelo's cross into his own net – as we strolled to a routine 4-0 victory.

Undoubtedly the star man had been De Bruyne, but most of the post-match comment and reporting again centred around Haaland, whose every touch had been scrutinised. And that wasn't the most demanding assignment, as he racked up just eight of them during his 74 minutes on the pitch. Guardiola was quick to defend his new man, asking, 'When you are a striker and teams like Bournemouth have three men at the back, two players in front and you are in the middle, how can you survive in that?' But in the sure knowledge that many others would employ similar tactics to neutralise Haaland, Pep was already thinking of how to adapt his team's style of play to integrate him more effectively into the side for when tougher challenges arrived. 'We'll find solutions. It's just a question of time.' A BBC graphic showed that Haaland had completed just two passes during the match, and one of those was a kick-off. Yet despite his minimal direct involvement in proceedings, he'd still delivered an assist with his other pass as well as being denied a certain goal when Foden chose to shoot from the angle rather than square the ball.

Still, while some pundits enjoyed themselves by almost mocking Haaland's lack of involvement, overlooking the fact that his movement had been a crucial factor in occupying defenders and creating space for others, it was a highly satisfactory day's work, made even sweeter for City fans enjoying a post-match pint when the news came through that United had shipped four first-half goals at Brentford. It meant that Erik ten Hag's brave new world had begun with his team at the bottom of the league. If Carlsberg did league tables …

Bournemouth had once again proved to be ideal opponents – City's Premier League record against them now reading played 11, won 11 – and Guardiola had taken the chance to use all his substitutes to get minutes into the legs of as many players as possible. But while the introductions of Grealish, Bernardo, Álvarez and Stones could have been anticipated, there was also a surprise when 17-year-old Rico Lewis came on to make his first-team debut, replacing Kyle Walker with ten minutes to go. He'd got a few minutes in friendlies during City's pre-season tour of the USA and the word was that Pep had seen something in the youngster that he really liked. Just how much he liked him would become apparent in the coming months.

Next up for City was a trip to St James' Park, to face a Newcastle side expected to show a big improvement this season after their change of ownership and substantial outlay on new players. There was plenty of distaste expressed about the source of their funding, and whether their Saudi owners were suitable inheritors of an institution steeped in the blameless history of our green and pleasant land. Welcome to the club. Like it or not, it's the future. Personally, I'd welcome the emergence of Newcastle as a serious force. The more competitive the league the better and if any set of fans had suffered enough it's theirs, many of their experiences mirroring our own before the money came in. Just like we did, they've stayed true to the cause through thin and thinner, and now it might be payback time.

Despite the waves of optimism coursing around the stadium, City began as though they were going to brush Newcastle aside, as they had so often in recent years, with İlkay Gündoğan quickly opening the scoring. But after half an hour there was a sweet moment for the Geordies and in particular for Miguel Almirón, who forced the ball home for a goal initially flagged as offside but correctly overturned by VAR. There was more than an element of karma about this – after the previous season's title-decider, that dramatic late win over Villa, Jack Grealish had joked to reporters that Riyad Mahrez had played like Almirón, an unnecessary, childish and embarrassing insult which was a bit rich coming from a player whose own contribution to our success had been so meagre. It would be surprising and disappointing if Pep hadn't given him a proper bollocking.

Even as a City fan it was hard not to feel pleased for Almirón, a man with one of the most winning smiles in football and whose performances as the season progressed would show Grealish just how wrong he was to make such belittling comments about a fellow professional. With the crowd as partisan as ever, Newcastle now had the bit between their teeth. Callum Wilson put them ahead before half-time and when Kieran Trippier extended the lead with a classic free kick, City were on the ropes.

But this is a team well accustomed to overcoming adversity. Within a few minutes Haaland reduced the arrears, crashing a loose ball home in emphatic style, and just four minutes later came a rather more refined goal, Kevin De Bruyne's precise and brilliantly subtle through ball being cleverly tucked away by Bernardo Silva. From then on City looked the more likely winners but couldn't find the decisive goal as a thrilling game ended all-square. Newcastle had been quite the revelation, and initial disappointment at the first dropped points of the season were tempered by the fact that this was clearly a side destined to cause problems for everyone they faced.

Next up is a home game against Palace, a team who'd enjoyed more than their fair share of success against City in recent years. It's a rare home game I'll have to miss, falling victim once again to that inexplicable phenomenon of friends getting married during the football season on a Saturday afternoon. At least Tom's a lifelong City fan, and he's already converted Maggie into a commendably enthusiastic Blue. But, honestly, can't you wait until the international break?

I've always been an unusually popular guest at weddings, unafraid and unashamed as I am to sit in a church with an earpiece tuned in to *Sport on Five* or, more recently, sneaking a look at a smartphone tucked neatly into the order of service. Being an atheist nutter probably helps. I've lost count of the number of literally just-married men who've walked back down the aisle arm-in-arm with their new bride and turned to me with a questioning glance or on occasion a more brazen 'what's the score?', prompting 'it'll never last' comments from those who don't understand. The best day of their lives? Only if their team wins.

At least this one isn't in a church and, just like the City-Palace game, it has a 3pm kick-off. As I half-listen to the usual proceedings, the grim tidings emerge that we've fallen behind via a John Stones own goal, and a few minutes later comes the scarcely credible news that we're two down, Andersen being allowed a free header from a corner. As I look ashen-faced at my mobile phone screen, the guy next to me asks 'City are two down?' with an evidently smug smirk on his face. I mutter something extremely uncharitable under my breath.

Half-time comes with Palace still two up and the interval is spent grabbing a taxi to take us to the reception. By the time we get there we've pulled a goal back through Bernardo, and I slip effortlessly into maximum unsociability mode, incapable of tearing myself away from my mobile phone. It's worth it though, as at regular ten-minute intervals news comes through of another City goal, three of them in total, all scored by Haaland. Tom's also evidently kept himself tuned in, for as he and Maggie arrive at the reception in an open-top car, he raises his hands to indicate a '4-2' signal to the waiting guests. If you know, you know.

It's the second consecutive time that we've recovered from two down – a point last week, all three this – mirroring the achievement in the final two games of last season. In all, that makes it four games in six that we've come back from a two-goal deficit and, while this shows a formidable fighting spirit, we do need to ask ourselves how we so frequently find ourselves in such a predicament to start with.

The next day's recorded highlights are enjoyable, but only because we already know the ending. Bernardo looked unplayable even in the first half, and there were several moments in the Palace area where ricochets could have fallen our way. But our defending for both Palace goals was abysmal, individual mistakes and lack of concentration, and the situation could and probably should have been even worse, with Palace having a goal disallowed when Ederson's attempted clearance was blocked by Édouard for Jordan

Ayew to roll home. Patrick Vieira doesn't make too much of a fuss about it afterwards but would have been well entitled to do so.

Instead, we get a bit of luck when Bernardo cuts into the Palace area from the left. There are nine Palace outfield players in the box as he does so, and his shot takes a slight deflection off one of them to flash low past Guaita and bring us back into the game. I already know what happens next but you can tell from the crowd's reaction that they do as well. We've been here before, and once that momentum shifts we're almost impossible to stop. Ten minutes later Foden brings a tricky ball under his spell and dinks an exquisite cross for Haaland to soar mightily and head home the equaliser.

It's all one way now, and some slick penalty area interplay leads to Stones's scuffed shot being turned home by an on-the-spot and exultant Haaland. The *coup de grâce* comes after Erling fastens on to Gündoğan's through ball and, despite the closest of close attention from Joel Ward, he holds him off to plant a composed finish past Guaita, complete a hat-trick and make the points safe. The goals have provided a great showcase of Erling's attributes – aerial prowess, Johnny on the spot and speed allied to strength. Nobody watching has the slightest doubt that this won't be the last time he gets to take home a match ball.

Pep inevitably faces a barrage of questions about Haaland, and is doubtless pleased when he gets the chance to talk about someone else. 'Bernardo Silva was a winning player today. He is the type of player that when the situation goes bad, he steps up. That's the biggest quality of a player. Everyone has skills, but how you react in the moments when the situation is wrong, he's maybe the best that we have.'

But with six goals in four games, there's only one player making the headlines. The man himself was very matter-of fact afterwards, saying, 'These games are why I'm here – to turn things around when there are difficult times,' while the BBC reported, 'Should he maintain his efficiency in front of goal, Haaland's ability to swing tight contests in City's favour is likely to prove an invaluable commodity in the title race.' Something of an understatement amid all the hype building up elsewhere.

14 September 2022, Champions League: City 2 Borussia Dortmund 1

'The moment he scored it,
I thought "Johan Cruyff"'

AFTER THAT dramatic, agonising 'Act of God' semi-final exit in Madrid, it was time for City to gird their loins for yet another attempt to win the Champions League. Year after year we'd been the bookies' favourites to bring home the trophy; year after year we'd found unlikely, dramatic and heartbreaking ways to fail. Away goals against Monaco after a 6-6 aggregate tie; a litany of refereeing decisions going against us against Liverpool, whose ostensibly comfortable 5-1 triumph was a gross misrepresentation of the play; the astonishing events against Spurs, with Raheem Sterling's late winner ruled out – correctly it must be said – for an offside decision that not one Spurs player had appealed for, coupled with Llorente's decisive goal being allowed because the VAR screen failed to show the referee the only angle from which the handball was clear; the spectator-less exit to a very average Lyon side, where some of the individual mistakes beggared belief; the defeat in the final against Chelsea, where for the only the second time in a

61-game season Pep sent out a team without either Rodri or Fernandinho; and finally that gut-wrenching episode in the Bernabéu, a defeat as sickening as it gets.

And so this season, the incentive couldn't be greater. Every pundit on planet Earth would trot out the same lazy assertion that City couldn't be considered to be one of the great sides until they won the Champions League. Although Pep tends to put it more politely, this is patently so much bollocks, but when you hear the same old drivel trotted out so many times, eventually you get bludgeoned into throwing in the towel and taking it as fact.

Pep's frequently lost it in press conferences with journalists who peddle this line, the essence of his argument being that the most important thing is to be there, to keep reaching the final stages and eventually your number will come up, you'll get the rub of the green in those critical moments. It's not a response that a lot of them like. So many journos, pundits and fans live in a binary world where it's win and you're fantastic, lose and you're rubbish. Every result is post-rationalised so that the winners always deserved to win, and the losers always deserved to lose. Hardly anyone uses the evidence of their own eyes anymore, it's all let's start from the result and construct the narrative from there, and the idea that luck plays a part in deciding tight games between two evenly matched teams is seen as preposterous. But it does. A lot. The only way to validate Pep's arguments is for us to lift the trophy, ideally in slightly fortuitous circumstances. And then, at last, we might shut people up.

This year's draw puts us in a group with Sevilla, Dortmund and Copenhagen. It could certainly be worse, but Dortmund are hardly a pushover while Sevilla's European pedigree – four recent Europa League titles – is something we can only dream of, even if they've never troubled the scorers in the Champions League.

And it's in Seville where we begin the campaign. On the face of it this is a tricky fixture, but never underestimate the importance of timing. It turns out that we're facing a side which has failed to win any of its first four games in La Liga, with manager Julen Lopetegui already under serious pressure. City's team in Andalusia features a new name – Manuel Akanji, signed from Borussia Dortmund on transfer deadline day for around £13m. He'd fallen out of favour at Dortmund, and a few eyebrows were raised when City came in for him. Dortmund fans were quick to express their feelings on social media, and most of them weren't too complimentary, the essence being 'thank you City for taking him off our hands'. Still, experience has taught us that Pep knows a bit more about football and footballers than the average supporter.

Sevilla, despite the backing of their famously partisan crowd, prove to be feeble opposition and City's first goal sums up their predicament. From our perspective it's brilliant, beautiful football, Foden receiving the ball on the right, waiting for De Bruyne to make an unchecked underlapping run and feeding a perfectly weighted pass into his path. We've created the overload with ease, and when Kev looks up he sees the Sevilla defenders all in a line on the edge of the six-yard box, giving him a clear path to fizz the ball into the space between them and the keeper. All he needs to do is execute, which he does, and hurtling in at the far post to prod the ball home is the inevitable Haaland. It's gorgeous football, but it's as if Sevilla have never watched us play before.

We squander a couple of other opportunities before Phil Foden takes centre stage in the second half. Some intricate footwork opens up a gap for him to fire a cleverly disguised shot into the corner, and a similar effort ten minutes later is parried by the keeper for the lurking Haaland to tap home. Game over, and Rúben Dias adds late gloss with a simple finish after excellent play from Cancelo. Akanji could hardly have had a more gentle start to his City career, but tougher tests surely lie ahead. Not least the next one, eight days later, when his old team come to the Etihad.

To say City fans' relationship with the Champions League has been difficult would be an understatement. The belief that UEFA was a corrupt organisation, that they had it in for City, was widespread and often so intense as to border on paranoia. Every dubious decision that went against us brought up the same old rhetoric, and the introduction of Financial Fair Play was seen as another way to keep us in our place, to prevent us from dining at the top table. UEFA's desire to protect the interests of a small number of historically important clubs irrespective of their current prowess is at the core of everything they do.

We began booing the Champions League anthem in 2012 and have never stopped since. The antipathy originated from a match in Porto when Mario Balotelli was racially abused by home supporters. Porto were fined €20,000. A month later, against Sporting Lisbon. City were fined €30,000 for being 30 seconds late coming on to the pitch for the second half. Next, when we were due to play CSKA Moscow away from home, the Russian club were belatedly ordered to play behind closed doors. That meant City fans couldn't attend the match either, even though thousands had already paid for flights, tickets and accommodation. No compensation was offered by UEFA and when the match took place, some 650 CSKA fans were then allowed into the stadium, thinly disguised as official representatives.

The following season, affronted at our habitual disrespect for their precious, pompous self-important pre-match walk-on music, UEFA charged us with a breach of their competition regulation 16.2, namely 'the disruption of national or competition anthems' after our home game against Sevilla. You couldn't make this stuff up. The return match in Spain saw many City fans stay silent, instead holding up placards with 'BOO!' written on them. UEFA eventually backed down, but had bigger things in mind, having already targeted us with their FFP regulations, designed specifically to protect their cartel of untouchables from unwelcome insurgent forces. Which by this stage basically meant us.

In the early days, City fans' derision carried over into the atmosphere when the match began. In addition, many season ticket holders chose not to purchase seats for Champions League games, meaning that their places were taken by day-trippers or simply left empty. Slowly, however, as the saga of trying to snare that elusive trophy has become ever more epic, more fans have embraced the competition. Most of us used to say that the Premier League was by far the most important thing to win, and some of us still do. But when you know how much the manager, the players, the whole club want to win this bloody thing, you can't help getting drawn into the crusade.

Pep has helped in this respect; after his initial plea for fans to stop booing the anthem was emphatically ignored, he accepted our right to do so and instead asked us to get fully behind the team once the whistle blew. And we have done, to the extent that the pre-match show of disdain serves as a prelude to an explosion of support. It's a bit like the well-established habit of relentless jeering as the United team sheet is read out ahead of derby games. Once it's over there's an eruption of noise and energy, as if that concerted burst of antagonism and contempt has served to gee the crowd up.

But on this particular occasion, City struggle to respond to the support. Dortmund are extremely well-organised and naturally have more idea than most about how to go about keeping Haaland quiet. Veteran defender Mats Hummels produces an accomplished display while Jude Bellingham, still only 19 despite having seemingly been around for ever, is a standout performer yet again. Their counterattacking play is superb, and they almost carve out a classic goal as Reus bends the ball just wide. City's reprieve is short-lived, and when Bellingham glances a header past Ederson no one is surprised. And no one can say they don't deserve it.

We're in trouble here all right, with several players struggling to make an impact, and none more so than Jack Grealish. Bereft of confidence, Jack is at his most timid and ineffective, and there are even some cheers when he's hooked after an hour. As the *Manchester Evening News* commented after the game, 'Grealish has lost the spark that made him such an exciting player at Aston Villa and now, a year on from his arrival, isn't looking any more accustomed to being in Guardiola's side.'

The introductions of Foden, Bernardo and Álvarez perk things up and City look far more threatening, with the crowd playing a full part in a way that they wouldn't have done a few years earlier. Some excellent football down the left sees Foden fire a low cross towards the marauding Haaland at the far post, but Hummels stretches desperately to toe the ball behind for a corner, and celebrates with his team-mates as though he's just scored a goal. Dortmund are seriously fired up but there's still more than ten minutes to go. And just a couple of them have elapsed when John Stones, taking up an ever more advanced role, controls a pass superbly and sets himself for a strike at goal from the corner of the penalty area. He catches it perfectly, and the ball flashes past the strangely motionless Alex Meyer into the near top corner.

Now it's all City, as the visitors focus on holding out for what would still be a great result. So when Cancelo gets the ball, some 40 yards out on the left, every single Dortmund player is between him and the goal. It looks as though there's nothing on. With the outside of his right foot, Cancelo fires in an angled cross towards the far post, at pace. They call it a 'trivela' apparently. It's a beautiful delivery. He's got form for this sort of thing and it's mightily impressive. Haaland moves towards the ball, but there are two defenders with him and the space between them is only a couple of yards. But launching himself upwards, he somehow elevates his left foot higher than the heads of his markers, and with impeccable timing deflects the ball into the net with his outer left ankle.

It's the sort of thing that you watch in real time and can't quite comprehend what's just happened. How did he do that? How could *anyone* do that? He refuses to celebrate in front of his former team-mates and fans – I know it's respectful but Jesus, when you've just scored a goal like that, how much self-restraint does it take? This guy is definitely not normal.

At the final whistle, there are warm embraces between Haaland and his erstwhile team-mates, most of whom can't help but laugh, or at least offer a wry smile, as they congratulate him. They've seen this sort of thing before. Their exchanges exude warmth and create the impression of genuine affection. The more we get to see him, the more it appears that as well as his prowess on the pitch, Erling is quite a difficult person to dislike.

Sky Sports' Adam Bate observed, 'Haaland's finish was reminiscent of a famous Cruyff goal for Barcelona against Atlético Madrid in 1973 – labelled the impossible goal – as he rose to volley the ball in at the far post. What is certain is that there are very few players in the game's history capable of the moments that this young man continues to produce.'

Pep certainly recognised the similarity. 'Maybe the people who know me know the influence of Johan Cruyff in my life as a person, a mentor, a manager. Years ago, he scored in Camp Nou an incredible goal versus Atlético Madrid. It was quite similar today with Haaland and the moment he scored it I thought, "Johan Cruyff".'

I'm old enough to vaguely remember Cruyff's goal and a quick search of YouTube reveals that it's been preserved for posterity. And watching the original again, there is indeed a real similarity. But Cruyff was almost balletic in his movement, so slim and supple, and it was no great surprise that he should be able to execute a feat of such gymnastic athleticism. Haaland is a six-foot-four monster, an absolute beast. For Cruyff to do it seemed natural; for Haaland to replicate it is almost supernatural.

Overall, however, it had not been a convincing display, and Pep acknowledged that the process of integrating Haaland into the side had barely even begun. We'd started out not adapting to the fact that we always had a presence in the box, but now it seemed as though we were looking for it all the time. 'Sometimes we want to rush so quick because Erling is there. You have this attraction of him, we want to attack it sometimes. We have to be more patient.'

But Kevin De Bruyne was relaxed enough. 'I think the way he has adapted to us is really good. Outside the goalscoring there is still another part of the game and I think that part is maybe more tough to adapt to. But it makes it more exciting. If he can adjust to the way we play there, then the level is going to go up. That's what we demand from him. He knows and we know we can still do better but that's only positive.'

Erling himself was all too well aware what people were saying about him, but while the good stuff didn't seem to go to his head, any perceived criticisms were like water off a duck's back, as he told Bein Sports. 'People maybe talk about that I don't touch the ball enough, but I don't care. I know what I'm going to do, what I have to do, and this is exactly what I'll keep doing … My dream is to touch the ball five times and score five goals.'

Pep's measured response is that he doesn't really like that particular objective, not that he'd be too upset if it was achieved. He knows that there's so much more he can get out of Haaland, to get him more involved in general play; the challenge will be to do it without compromising his extraordinary ability to make the hardest part of the game look so simple.

4

2 October 2022, Premier League: City 6 Manchester United 3

'Not in my lifetime? Now it's every time!'

NEWLY PROMOTED Nottingham Forest were the next Premier League visitors to the Etihad, and it came as no surprise when they set up with a low block. But they didn't do it very well, and their attempts to frustrate City were futile. Well before half-time Haaland had completed another hat-trick, all dispatched with minimal fuss from close range, all of them the culmination of brilliant, inventive attacking play. And this was a lesson that sitting deep with numbers at the back isn't in itself sufficient to deal with Haaland. You might be able to deny him the opportunity to run in behind you, but his movement in short spaces, instinctive positioning and physical strength allow him to prosper even in the most crowded of penalty areas. His first goal in particular emphasised how difficult it is to stop him, as he sprinted to get to the near post to meet Foden's diagonal cross and despite Joe Worrall having a fistful of his shirt, meet an awkward bouncing ball with the outside of his foot to turn it instantly past Dean Henderson. You have to work so hard not just to deny him space but also to cut off the supply line, and here Forest could do neither.

Pep had insisted from the start of the season that Julián Álvarez wasn't merely an understudy and occasional alternate for Haaland; the two of them could play together. And here they did so to great effect, the Argentine operating slightly behind Erling and producing a highly encouraging performance, rewarded with two second-half goals. They weren't important in the context of the game – the final two in a 6-0 rout – but the way they were taken was impressive, the second displaying an explosive power which had a familiar feel to it. Comparisons with Sergio had started even before Álvarez arrived here, and this early demonstration of clinical ruthlessness didn't do anything to quieten them. But suggestions that he might prove to be an absolute steal at £17m were swamped by the deluge of headlines surrounding the striking Viking. With nine goals in his first five games, Haaland had now set a new record for the number of goals at this stage of a Premier League season. Another utterly meaningless stat, and there'd be plenty more where that came from.

Next it was off to Aston Villa, to face a side managed by Steven Gerrard, now synonymous with two so near and yet so far title near misses for Liverpool. His 2014 slippery moment at Anfield opened the door for Manuel Pellegrini's men and then, four months ago, when his Villa side were close to diverting the Premier League trophy to Jürgen Klopp, Silky İlkay ensured that the afternoon ended with the increasingly familiar sight of tears among the Anfield faithful.

City fans are quick to remind Gerrard of his fateful Demba Ba moment, while watching Villa play like an away side at home. They make a much better fist of keeping things tight than Forest did, but are eventually worn down early in the second half when De Bruyne's immaculate cross from the right takes out Martínez and is turned home athletically on the volley by the leaping Haaland.

City create further chances but can't get the second goal, and Villa are rewarded for staying in the game when their first shot on target, a sweet first-time effort from Leon Bailey, leaves Ederson helpless. It could have become even worse, the referee responding to the linesman's flag by blowing for offside against Philippe Coutinho, a second before the Brazilian reminded us of his Anfield pomp by bending a 20-yarder into the top corner. We've seen that sort of thing far too often over the years, and it's a relief that it came just after the whistle – especially when replays show that Coutinho had actually been onside. We definitely got away with one there, although it would have been a complete misrepresentation of the play had Villa taken the points.

The next league game was also in the Midlands, against a Wolves side struggling for form with manager Bruno Lage clinging on to his job by a thread. Last season this had been one of the great nights, with Kevin De Bruyne racking up four goals in an unforgettable 5-1 win which took us to the cusp of the title. It was a stunning performance from Kev and the team as a whole, especially coming just a week after that horrific night in Madrid.

And we carried on here as we'd finished then, taking the lead after 55 seconds. De Bruyne was once again heavily involved, in a move that may have been familiar but was still proving difficult for opponents to counter. Lovely interplay down the right saw Foden release Kev with a cute back-heel, and his crisp low cross was straight into Haaland territory. This time, however, the big man couldn't reach it but steaming in behind him, busting a gut to get into the six-yard box, was Jack Grealish, who held off the tracking defender to stretch and plant the ball home.

It was Jack's first of the season, and we all hoped it would ignite a spark in him. Our second was also unusual, not in the scorer but in the manner of the goal, as Haaland picked up the ball 30 yards out, went on a weaving run, then fired a low 20-yarder into the corner. It was Erling's first of the season from outside the box, and would also be the last.

City's task was made easier when a Nigel de Jong-style challenge from Nathan Collins saw him plant his studs into Grealish's midriff, but Wolves played rather better with ten men and, as Pep would say afterwards, the next goal looked more likely to bring the score back to 2-1 rather than put us out of sight. Instead, some more clever interplay down the right allowed us to get a man over, and again that man was De Bruyne. Another low cross saw Foden get ahead of his marker to execute a delicate flick into the far corner, and seal an ultimately comfortable win.

September had passed without City having had even one Premier League fixture at the Etihad – a combination of the international break and the postponement of the Tottenham game due to the passing of the Queen. It was difficult to understand why the natural-causes death of a 96-year old woman two days earlier should force all of the weekend's football to be postponed. Would fans up and down the land have been too distraught to come out to watch their team? Wouldn't a couple of minutes' silence have sufficed, given that there'd be plenty of opportunity to mourn for those who wished to do so? Pubs and restaurants were still open, people were out and about, smiling and laughing in public, so why couldn't we go to the football? Was the whole football-watching population expected just to sit indoors and wallow in misery?

The potential implications of the postponements in this of all seasons were significant. It would have been bad enough anyway but with the schedule from January onwards even more congested than usual, there wouldn't be enough midweek slots to fit in all the games in the event that City went all the way in the cup competitions. But that was something to worry about if and when the situation arose: a much more pressing matter was the imminent Manchester derby.

After their disastrous start to the Erik ten Hag tenure – a home defeat by Brighton followed by that 4-0 pasting at Brentford – United's results had picked up, sparked by a win over a pitifully limp Liverpool at Old Trafford. They then managed to beat early pacesetters Arsenal, hitting them on the counterattack despite having enjoyed little of the play, and they arrived at the Etihad on the back of four straight wins. There was a sense that their results had generally been better than the performances, but there were plenty prepared to talk up their chances, especially with their recent record at the Etihad being remarkably good – we'd managed just two wins in their previous eight visits.

The team news wasn't encouraging, with Rodri having suffered a rare injury and, with Kalvin Phillips injured, Gundo had to slot in as our holding midfielder. Whenever Rodri's absent for a big game I automatically think 'Champions League Final against Chelsea' and break out into a cold sweat. With Dias also absent, on the bench with a central defensive pairing of Aké and Akanji preferred, it felt as though the spine of our team was seriously weakened.

Most of us expected United to come and play what Manuel Pellegrini used to call 'cowards' football', sitting back and hoping to nick a goal or two on the counter. Pep is never quite so disparaging, at least not in public, and talked up United before the match, in particular the danger they posed on transitions. And without Rodri, those transitions would be more threatening than ever.

City are aggressive, enterprising and dominant from the off. Within two minutes, Dalot is yellow-carded for a foul on Grealish, after which a flurry of shots rain in on the United goal, as City swarm all over their visitors. When the breakthrough comes in only the eighth minute it already seems overdue, but it's certainly worth the wait. Bernardo zips a low ball into Foden, just short of the near post, and with supreme technique the Stockport Iniesta wraps his left foot around it to whip an unstoppable shot in at De Gea's near post. Foden had scored an almost identical goal at Stamford Bridge a couple of years previously – I can't off the top of my head think of a goal of similar technique from any other player. He's one of our own, and one on his own.

The crowd are already pumped up, and there's no holding back from City as United's midfield is bypassed time and again. Like all teams City are sometimes guilty of sitting back for a period after getting a breakthrough, but here they're like a pack of wolves, hunting down the ball whenever United have possession and creating chances almost at will. Another flowing move ends with a Foden snapshot from around the penalty spot, but the ball fizzes just wide when most inside the Etihad are up on their feet ready to celebrate. Gündoğan's free kick leaves De Gea stranded but crashes on to the outside of the post, then De Bruyne's drive is tipped on to the bar and over by the keeper's fingertips.

It's an onslaught, but United are still hanging on until the resulting corner curls into the goalmouth. Haaland already had a good six-inch start over his alleged markers, but his prodigious leap makes him look like a giant among pygmies as he powers his header goalwards. Malacia hooks the ball away but Michael Oliver's watch tells the story we all want to hear, as he points to the centre spot.

And now there's no stopping us, as the half's remaining ten minutes see us produce two of the great derby goals. Moving down his favoured inside-right channel – or at least that's what folk of my vintage call it – De Bruyne delivers one of those low, curling diagonal crosses which passes behind the United defenders as it skips off the turf. It's aimed at Haaland, but from my angle, right behind the line of the delivery, it's just too far ahead of him. 'That was almost perfect,' I think to myself, just as Haaland launches himself horizontally, thrusts out a seemingly telescopic left leg and studs the ball past a startled De Gea. And there are thousands of us just as startled as the United keeper. I turn round to the guys behind me, and we're all almost lost in wonder. 'How the hell did he reach that?' But he did. It's what he does. It's not quite as spectacular as his gravity-defying effort against Dortmund but it's not far off. What sort of specimen have we got on our hands here?

As if this extraordinary display of finishing isn't enough, Haaland's next contribution is to provide a scarily realistic Kevin De Bruyne impression. Fed by the real KDB's incisive pass down the left, he sprints on to the ball while looking up to see what's available in the box. And rapidly becoming available is Phil Foden, who's nearing the end of an 80-yard sprint to the far post. He's been tracked all the way by Malacia, but Haaland's low cross is inch-perfect and Foden, displaying the pace which seems to have improved year by year, gets there first to slide the ball home for a wonderful goal.

'Foden two, Haaland two ... United nothing at all,' says Peter Drury, while Guy Mowbray's commentary over the image of a bewildered Alex Ferguson is simply beautiful. In dragging up a famous quote from the old tyrant and adding his own embellishment, Mowbray produced a classic of his own. 'Alex Ferguson was asked in 2009 whether Manchester City could ever go into a derby as favourites. He said, "Not in my lifetime." Now it's every time!'

This is attacking play from the gods, some of the most exhilarating football ever seen at the Etihad. Over on Sky Sports, the superlatives are flowing both from Martin Tyler – 'It's from the pages of schoolboy fiction this. When do you see football like this. Breathtaking, brilliant!' – and even, albeit through gritted teeth, co-commentator Gary Neville. 'Let's be absolutely clear … this is sensational. Out of this world. You've just got to admire and respect that that is an absolutely brilliant goal. Manchester United are getting an absolute doing.'

Half-time comes shortly afterwards, and United can count themselves lucky to be only four down. As Sky cut to the adverts, cameras outside the ground feast on the sight of their fans streaming out of the stadium, while inside the studio the fire brigade are put on red alert as Roy Keane is on the verge of spontaneous combustion. He slates the whole team, and Eriksen gets a proper pasting for his failure to track runners or at least bring them down. Doubtless United would have been better served had Casemiro been available, although there's equally every chance he'd have been sent off by now.

The second half begins with Foden's angled shot being turned away by De Gea, but with the game so clearly already won, there's a marked drop in the team's intensity. Much as it would be lovely to put eight past these, there's a Champions League game on Wednesday and energy conservation is paramount. Antony, another of these Flash Harry, more style than substance 'all about me' wingers that United so seem to love, fastens on to a ball that Grealish really should have cut out – though it's churlish to criticise him, as he's been excellent so far and at the heart of the early forays . which so unsettled the United defence – and cuts inside before delivering a 25-yarder which curls into Ederson's far corner.

It's bloody irritating, and initially makes me uncomfortable. I still can't shake off those insecurities built up over decades of incompetence – 'What if they score another, then another, then another?' – but my paranoia is soon put away for another day when Sergio Gómez, signed from Anderlecht late in the transfer window and on for the injured Kyle Walker, is freed down the left. He drills a precise low ball into the heart of the area and Haaland's left-footed shot is timed perfectly, clipping the ball at pace past De Gea to complete a supreme hat-trick. The goal puts me in mind of Sergio Agüero's winner in the 2014 home derby, and if Erling carries on scoring at this rate then he won't have to stay too long for Sergio's record goal tally to come under threat.

We're back in the comfort zone, and extra gloss soon arrives as Foden finds space in the area to side-foot the ball past De Gea with some aplomb. The celebrations are muted, as Phil looked offside, but after the usual delay while the bumbling technophobes in Stockley Park draw the relevant lines, the goal is awarded to allow him to register a hat-trick of his own. It's 6-1, a scoreline enshrined in all our hearts and, just as on that occasion, it should have been ten. Already.

There's plenty of time to heap more pain on the smattering of United fans still in the stadium, but with 15 minutes left, Pep makes a raft of substitutions and the subsequent proceedings become somewhat disjointed. United manufacture the odd chance and then a thrust down the left results in Martial heading home. In added time, an infuriatingly clumsy and unnecessary challenge from Cancelo gifts United a penalty, which Martial calmly dispatches to complete the afternoon's activity.

Despite having battered our detested rivals, City fans leave the ground with an initial sense of disappointment – a 6-3 scoreline makes the game sound like a reasonably closely fought nine-goal thriller rather than the brutal demolition it's actually been. Even so, the feeling soon wears off as we fete the unique achievement of two derby hat-tricks, both from 22-year-olds. With Haaland also racking up two assists, it's a bonanza week for the millions who'd chosen him as their Fantasy League captain, and a demonstration of how he's more than just a goalscorer.

In *The Times*, there was no question of allowing the scoreline to mislead. 'Two late goals superficially gave United's effort some respectability, but everyone here at the Etihad knows they witnessed a humiliation,' said Henry Winter, adding, 'City aren't even top of the league, yet it feels like the title race is over.' In the *Daily Telegraph*, Jason Burt brought out the old 'demolition derby' cliche, adding that United's three goals represented 'an astonishing anomaly'. And what a depressing day it was for some of the pundits.

Roy Keane: 'I am shocked at how poor United have been. It is brilliant from City but it's like the game is too big for Manchester United. The occasion has got too big for them. They should be embarrassed. But City were magnificent. Watching them live is a pleasure, they are one of the best teams I've ever seen.'

Gary Neville: 'In the first half United froze. There's no doubt they bottled it. There has been promise in the last few weeks but this was a reminder how far behind the best team in the country they actually are' He predicted that 'City will win the league by between 15 and 20 points'.

Pep tried his best to dampen down the euphoria. 'Some players were not good today and have to improve. Perfection doesn't exist, it's impossible. But we have to look for it. We have done well today but we can do better. Many, many players made sloppy passes and this is not good.' He's a hard taskmaster all right.

For Foden, the sky's the limit – it always has been – and for a born and bred Blue to get his first senior hat-trick in a Manchester derby seems almost too good to be true. And he's still a work-in-progress, a player continuing to learn the role of a central creative midfielder, the position where he'll surely end up. But wherever he plays on pitch, he's always had a great instinct for sniffing out goalscoring opportunities, and what a day for him to demonstrate it to the full.

And yet, with three consecutive home Premier League hat-tricks and goals in every away game so far, Haaland's tally of 14 goals in just eight games seems to be the only topic in town. 'We have a goalscoring machine up-front,' İlkay Gündoğan says. 'He has the smell for where the ball is going to drop, for the danger and he has shown that incredibly in the first few games. That was not a surprise to me. A little surprise was maybe just the way he is. He is sitting in the dressing room next to me and I see his behaviour from very close and he has just the right mind-set … It's not just the goals – it's the character and attitude he shows every single day.'

Pep again, 'The quality we have alongside him helps him score, but what he is doing I didn't teach him. He has incredible instincts. It comes from his mum and dad. He was born with that.' Add in his goals in Europe and he's already netted 17 in ten – and to emphasise Pep's point about instinct, 15 of them have been executed with a single touch. Right time, right place, perfect body positioning to allow him to strike instantly and an almost supernatural athleticism have combined to produce a player unlike anything the Premier League has seen before. If the sky's the limit for Phil, where the hell is this guy going to end up?

5

16 October 2022, Premier League: Liverpool 1 City 0

'All game it was play on and play on.
Except the goal'

CITY FOLLOW up the thrashing of United with a clinical dismissal of FC Copenhagen, seen off 5-0 with just the two more goals for Haaland. Southampton are next for the treatment and Foden's hot streak continues. Early on he plays a gorgeous crossfield pass to put Erling away, and the striker confidently clips the ball past Bazunu, first-time, of course. We're all out of our seats to celebrate yet another Haaland goal and there's a sense of disbelief when the ball strikes the inside of the post and rebounds to safety. The machine is human after all.

But Phil's soon creating again, setting Cancelo off on a mazy run which ends with a fierce low shot to register City's opener. I'm really not sure that this guy should be playing as a defender. Foden then executes a gorgeous dinked finish to double the lead after fastening on to De Bruyne's pass, with Haaland dragging defenders away to create the crucial space. Second-half goals from Mahrez and – what took him so long? – Big Erl complete the scoring in the most routine of victories.

It had been a fabulous week for the team – 15 goals in three games and some supreme individual performances – but now came the acid test. A trip to Anfield, where our record is beyond wretched. Just two wins since 1981, and one of those was in an empty stadium. Yes, that 4-1 victory back in 2021 was one to savour, capped by Foden's wondrous strike for the final goal, but that wasn't really winning at Anfield. Winning at Anfield requires taking on that unique crowd which time and again in the modern era has served to intimidate the Blues and inspire Liverpool to success, even when they've been on the ropes for much of the game. Several times City have travelled to Anfield as favourites to win, every time failing to do so, occasionally due to misfortune but usually because they couldn't cope with the occasion and atmosphere, and the way Klopp's men responded to it.

And today, we're perhaps the strongest favourites we've ever been. While we could hardly be in better form, Liverpool have struggled for consistency in a fashion not witnessed by a Klopp team for several years. With just ten points from eight games, they're already a full 13 points behind us, albeit with a game in hand, and there are many suggesting that their title challenge is already over. It almost certainly will be if they lose today.

The sight of James Milner at right-back could only have boosted City's confidence still further – in the previous year's fixture Foden and Bernardo led him a merry dance and there was widespread amazement that he didn't receive a second yellow card at a crucial stage of the game. Anywhere but Anfield. That game had ended in a thrilling 2-2 draw, City's clear superiority on the day offset by two moments of pure brilliance from Salah.

From the start it's a fiercely contested and feisty game – no surprises there. Referee Anthony Taylor is determined to keep the action moving, allowing challenges from both sides to go unpunished when most would have expected a free kick to be awarded. City don't appear to be going at it full throttle in an attacking sense, mindful of Liverpool's threat on the counter, but with Klopp's men having struggled so much defensively it's a little disappointing that we can't create more than a couple of half-chances, the best of which sees Haaland direct a powerful angled header straight at Alisson.

The big flashpoint – and there always seems to be one in this fixture – comes when Haaland shrugs off Fabinho's challenge, then forces the ball through Alisson's hands for Foden to squeeze it home. The celebrations from both Foden and the City fans in the Anfield Road End are as intense as it gets, but the Liverpool players surround the referee, pleading for the goal to be disallowed. At first, it seems as though their objections relate to the challenge on Alisson, but as TV replays wind back the footage it becomes clear that Haaland had taken a fistful of Fabinho's shirt before breaking free. Taylor is duly sent to the VAR monitor and rules in Liverpool's favour, to Guardiola's absolute disgust, and as he turns to remonstrate with anyone within earshot he gets pelted with coins from Liverpool supporters.

Taken in isolation, Haaland had committed an obvious foul, but in the context of this particular game, with Taylor having let several similar incidents go – and some arguably even worse – it was easy to see why Pep was so enraged. The VAR officials could hardly be criticised for calling Taylor to the monitor, but Guardiola's argument was that for Taylor to then take their side was inconsistent with every decision he'd previously made. But once they've been sent to the screen, it's rare indeed to find a referee brave enough to stick to their original call.

The incident and its outcome bring Liverpool fans to a frenzy, and signal a shift in momentum of a game in which we'd generally looked comfortable, albeit seldom posing a real threat. City temporarily become distracted, and are all over the place when a cross finds the unmarked Jota, who heads a great chance into the side-netting. Then Salah races away, and attempts to slide the ball past Ederson. The keeper gets the faintest touch to shift the ball's direction from an inch inside the post to an inch outside it. It's a scarily close shave, Ederson's intervention so slight that the referee doesn't even notice it and awards a goal kick.

City aren't without their own threat as the game opens up, with Haaland's low shot forcing a fingertip save from Alisson. It feels like we're getting on top again, and when we get a free kick in a perfect position for De Bruyne to whip in a dangerous cross, the area is flooded with bodies. Liverpool leave Salah upfield, with only Cancelo for company.

De Bruyne's delivery is an absolute shocker, allowing Alisson not only to claim the ball with ease, but also affording him the time to drill a low clearance towards Salah, with Cancelo in close attendance. Rather than ensuring that he gets something on the ball, Cancelo tries to bring it under control but instead misses it completely, and an extraordinary first touch from the Egyptian sends him away one-on-one with Ederson, with no one else in the vicinity. As with Thierry Henry back in the day, the keeper can see what Salah's going to do but has no chance of stopping him, as the ball is passed sweetly past Eddie into the Kop end net.

It was a shocking mistake from Cancelo, but clearly also a major tactical risk to have left him so exposed to such an outcome. And it was enough to decide the game, with a frustrated City unable to create a subsequent chance of note against a pumped-up side – although, hardly for the first time, not quite so pumped up as their manager, who received a red card for his furious complaints after Salah was denied a free kick.

There are plenty of City fans who detest Klopp, but I'm certainly not among them. Yes, he's over-exuberant at times and his leaping on to the pitch celebrations of a few years ago were massively over the top. And his protestations about Liverpool being poor relations when it comes to spending in the transfer market are hardly borne out by the facts. But if you can't appreciate what his teams have produced – first at Dortmund and then at Anfield – then football really isn't the game for you. Back in 2012, his Dortmund side gave what I still consider to be the best away performance I've ever seen at the Etihad, repeatedly carving Roberto Mancini's league champions apart only to come up against Joe Hart's finest ever City display, as we somehow mustered a 1-1 draw.

His 'heavy metal football' may be poles apart from Pep's more considered, precise, sophisticated approach but it's based on going at the opposition with pace, intensity and skill and were it not for the extraordinary and unprecedented points totals amassed by City in recent years would have yielded at least another couple of Premier League titles. It's a bit like the Federer/Nadal/Djokovic rivalry in tennis – in a sense, they're unlucky to have been playing at the same time and would all have won many more Grand Slams had the others not been around. But each of them pushed the others to new heights, and to play at a level which they otherwise wouldn't have attained. The 2019 and 2022 title races were arguably the two most thrilling and accomplished in history, with City winning their last 14 in 2019 – and having to, or else the title would have gone – before launching another extraordinary unbeaten run in 2022. It's been a truly great rivalry so far, and you can make a pretty strong case for it being the one of the highest quality.

Can't say I have anything like the same feelings about much of the Liverpool support, however, with their 'divine right' mentality mirroring that of the more recently fallen giants at Old Trafford. Their sense of entitlement is nauseating. Let's be honest, we'll go into decline at some time or other, maybe very soon, but when we do I hope our fans deal with it rather better than those of these two have done.

Pep's still seething after the game. On being asked about the disallowed goal he simply stated, 'This is Anfield. The referee spoke with me and Jürgen and said that he wasn't going to blow for fouls unless they were clear, and all game it was play on, and play on, and play on, and play on. Except for the goal.' And he wasn't too enamoured with the Liverpool fans, who'd pelted him with coins after the disallowed goal. 'Next time they will do it better. They didn't get me. They tried but didn't get me.' Then, referring to the unprovoked attack on the team coach before the Champions League game in 2018, he said, 'They got at the coach years ago, but not this time.' Pep remembers. We all remember.

You could already guess the next day's headlines – Liverpool kickstart their season – and they may well have done. They're way behind us – and even further behind Arsenal – but they're the only other team with a proven track record of generating win after win after win, and nobody should be stupid enough to rule them out. The only consolation we can take is that at least the season's worst fixture is out of the way.

6

2 November 2022, Champions League: City 3 Sevilla 1

'We don't give out presents here'

AFTER HAALAND'S acrobatic brilliance had delivered that important win over Dortmund, the next European assignment looked rather less demanding, a home game against FC Copenhagen. The Danes were out of the game by the half-hour, with two Haaland goals causing Pep to turn to his backroom staff, shake his head and smile. Even he seemed to be wondering, 'How does this guy always seem to find himself in the right place?'

The only disappointment for the crowd was that Erling was taken off at half-time, denying us the opportunity to witness yet another hat-trick, but this was becoming a common occurrence as City sought to manage his game time, mindful of his previous injury record. With the group-stage schedule severely compressed due to the impending World Cup, the return fixture took place in Copenhagen just six days later.

This time, with City almost qualified, Haaland was left on the bench but we still started as though the game would be another formality.

After ten minutes, Rodri moved on to a lay-off from Julián Álvarez and leathered a stunning 25-yarder, straight as an arrow, into the far top corner. What a way to chalk up your first Champions League goal. As the players and away fans continued to celebrate and Copenhagen prepared to restart, the referee suddenly made the dreaded VAR signal and came over to the monitor. Amid general mystification, he indicated that the goal had been disallowed for handball, an offence so indiscernible that not one Copenhagen player had appealed for it. It transpired that, in falling from the sky, the ball had accidentally brushed Mahrez's hand, before he flicked it away for Álvarez to tee up Rodri. And even though this minimal and obviously accidental contact had in no way helped Riyad control the ball, it was enough for the goal to be disallowed. Rodri would thus have to wait to open his Champions League account, and it was hard to imagine him doing it in a way as memorable as tonight would have been. But you never know.

Shortly afterwards another VAR intervention, another hard-to-credit handball decision for which not one player appeals and this time a penalty to City. Mahrez steps up and strikes the ball well enough, but keeper Grabara pulls off a great save, which serves to ramp up the atmosphere. Suddenly they're really up for this.

A rare Copenhagen break sees their striker get in a bit of a tangle with Sergio Gómez, but the referee waves play on. This time there are appeals, lots of them from players and crowd, and after another inordinate delay, the referee trots off once again to the pitchside monitor. He's spent so much time there that they ought to install a comfy chair for him to sit in. Gómez, correctly, is shown the red card and City face the prospect of an hour's football with ten men.

They manage the handicap well enough, coming away with a goalless draw which confirms qualification.

On the flight home, I've taken my place when a chap asks if he can get through to the seat inside me. He's wearing a sweatshirt with the official UEFA logo on it. I reply, 'Not if you had anything to do with disallowing that Rodri goal last night.' He smiles and strenuously denies any responsibility, telling me that he's in charge of stadium branding on Champions League nights. Like pretty well everyone else apart from those with a vested interest, he's no fan of VAR and particularly the interpretation of what constitutes handball.

I say, 'I wish they'd just left it at goal-line technology, at least that's something you can trust,' but he tells me not to be so sure. The cameras are fixed precisely in place on the stand, looking along the goal line but he says that in windy conditions there can sometimes be indiscernible but potentially significant movement. Of course, the tiniest change in angle would be amplified over the 30 yards or so to the goalposts, and even a few millimetres can make a match-changing difference. My mind flicks back to the John Stones clearance against Liverpool in the seismic 2019 encounter, where just 12mm of the ball was deemed not to have crossed the line. But then I don't recall it being particularly windy that night, so it must have been the right decision.

Next we're off to Dortmund, with City needing a point to top the group and Dortmund needing a point to qualify. That the game ended goalless would have surprised absolutely no one, but there were plenty of near-misses until the teams gradually agreed to settle for a draw. From City's perspective, there were several concerns. Haaland's return to his old club was curtailed at half-time, with a foot injury

– 'nothing serious' according to Pep – prompting a safety-first substitution. João Cancelo also failed to reappear for the second half, having been given a proper chasing by Dortmund's Karim Adeyemi. Cancelo's creativity has been a huge asset, but his defensive fallibility – at times it appears that he doesn't take that part of his game seriously, not ideal for a man nominally selected as a full-back – shows no sign of receding.

But the game's most headline-worthy incident was another missed penalty from Riyad Mahrez. He went for the other corner from his unsuccessful effort at Copenhagen, but again the ball was struck at what Barry Davies was fond of calling 'a height that the goalkeeper would appreciate' and Gregor Kobel pulled off a fine save. It was Mahrez's third failure in the last four attempts and continues City's less-than-stellar record from the spot, whoever the taker might be. The recent downturn in Riyad's success rate follows a much more successful phase, in which he put away some crucially important spot-kicks. But he'll always be remembered for the first one he took for City, when he blazed over the bar very late on at Anfield with the game still goalless. This was the season which ended with our 14-match winning run to hold Liverpool at bay, and as the pressure built week by week, every match needing to be won, his penalty miss was brought up again and again by the fans. 'If only Mahrez, had scored at Anfield … that miss could cost us the league.'

Of course it was one of many incidents that might have gone on to cost us the league, but the fact that it was against our direct rivals, and that Mahrez had taken the ball away from Gabriel Jesus and apparently insisted on taking the penalty, was a definite black mark in his relationship with City supporters. In reality, Pep had sent instructions over for Riyad to take the kick, given his impressive penalty practice in training. All was well that ended well, with Mahrez almost symbolically scoring the crucial third goal at Brighton on the final day, and yet the memory of that Anfield miss remained, for some fans, a stick to beat him with.

Guardiola has always defended those who miss penalties, citing the personality and courage needed to step up to take them in the first place, but this was becoming a bit much. Papers dug up the stats, revealing that City had missed 25 of 80 penalties since Pep arrived, nine more failures than would have been expected if they'd attained the average success rate of four out of five. It's a significant difference, and Pep acknowledges its importance. 'Since I've been here we've missed 25 penalties. It's too many. You always have to admire the courage, but missing so many is a problem. We have to improve. It comes down to fine margins in this competition and these situations can make the difference.' And with the abolition of the away goals rule increasing the likelihood of City becoming embroiled in a Champions League shoot-out at some stage, the importance of that difference can't be underestimated.

City's final group game was a dead rubber, at home to Sevilla, and a great chance to give minutes to players whose appearances had so far been restricted. Stefan Ortega, Sergio Gómez and Cole Palmer are all given starts, with Álvarez replacing the still-recuperating Haaland. But the left-field selection was a first senior start for Rico Lewis at right-back. An academy product, local lad, and still a few weeks short of his 18th birthday, Lewis had made a couple of brief substitute appearances in Premier League games, but this was a different proposition. Dead rubber or not, his inclusion as a starter rather than a late substitute sent a message that here was a player that Pep had enormous trust in.

It quickly became apparent that Lewis would be playing in a hybrid role, moving up into midfield when City had possession which, as usual, was most of the time. And his team-mates clearly had absolute faith in him, never reluctant to pass to him even when space was tight, and he kept moves flowing with a composure well beyond his years. However, City's general performance lacked a cutting edge and they went in at half-time a goal down, having conceded a header direct from a corner.

Early in the second half, Lewis, evidently being given licence to push forward, surged down the right on to a cute ball from Álvarez and with most in the crowd – as well as goalkeeper Yassine Bounou – expecting a cut-back across goal, he side-footed the ball high past the keeper at the near post. Rico's expression of youthful exuberance was a joy to behold, as was that of Academy standard-bearer Phil Foden as he rushed across to congratulate him. It was a record-breaking goal, making Lewis the youngest player to score a Champions League goal on his full debut. But he's still only City's second-youngest European scorer – I was stood on the Kippax back in March 1970 when Tony Towers blasted home the winner against Académica de Coimbra in the last minute of extra time and it's a memory that will stay with me for ever.

City were now treating the game as a properly competitive fixture, illustrated by the introduction of Kevin De Bruyne 20 minutes from time. And almost immediately, Kev registered an assist which even by his stellar standards was something special, a perfectly weighted diagonal ball threaded through for Álvarez to surge on to, before rounding the keeper to drill the ball home. Álvarez completed another impressive display by hounding José Carmona into an error, dispossessing him to play Mahrez in for an emphatic finish. Rico would understandably get all the headlines – plus his very own standing ovation on being substituted with a couple of minutes to go – but Álvarez had been outstanding once more and De Bruyne; well, what else was there to say?

Pep was full of praise for Rico, saying, 'We see him every day, we don't give out presents here. Not just because he's a Manchester City fan and from the Academy, he has to earn it. But we've known since day one that this guy has something special. He's aggressive enough defensively but does have a lot of margin to improve and with the ball when playing inside he is so good.' And with one half spent playing inside, the second out wide, it was indeed his use of the ball and strength which caught the eye on what would have been a seriously noteworthy debut even without the goal.

Pep also compliments the Academy, listing a few of the players who'd come through the system. But for all the success, with its teams routinely winning competitions across all age groups, the fact remains that only Phil Foden has cemented himself as a member of the squad likely to start in the biggest of games. Others, the likes of Jadon Sancho, Brahim Díaz, and more recently Roméo Lavia have chosen to leave and get first-team football elsewhere and while he'd have been happy for them all to stay, Pep's not going to beg. 'If they are not patient and they listen more to what the agents say then they can leave.' It'll be a surprise to see Rico going anywhere soon, though.

7

5 November 2022, Premier League: City 2 Fulham 1

*'It was one of the best
experiences we've had here'*

AFTER LOSING their unbeaten record at Anfield, City found themselves four points behind Arsenal, whose tremendous start to the season was showing no sign of letting up. No one, least of all Gooners, thought they'd be good enough to keep going and take the title, as recent years had only served to prove that at least one of Alex Ferguson's alleged pearls of wisdom was correct – the season doesn't really start until you get into March. That's when the pressure ratchets up, and when pretenders are undone. Unless they're Leicester. Even so, City certainly could do without falling further behind, and with four favourable-looking fixtures before the World Cup break, maximum points were expected.

The first of them brought Brighton to the Etihad. Guardiola is routinely fulsome in his praise of opposition teams and managers ahead of each match – 'they pose an incredible threat' being a stock phrase – but in the case of Brighton and Roberto De Zerbi he really pushed the boat out. Under Graham Potter, the Seagulls had played some excellent football but were frequently let down by the lack of a cutting edge. Potter's departure to Chelsea opened the door for De Zerbi to come across from Shakhtar Donetsk, but in terms of results – no wins in his first four games – the new man had got off to a poor start. Even so, Pep talked his abilities up, and over the coming months the rest of the football world would see why.

Alisson's assist for Salah's decisive goal at Anfield had shown that the ultimate Route One tactic can still be a pretty effective weapon and, with Haaland's extreme pace, it was just a matter of time before Ederson added to his own tally. Today was the day. His drilled clearance saw the rampaging striker sprint forward, barge Adam Webster out of the way while simultaneously rounding keeper Robert Sánchez, then calmly roll the ball into the net. Brighton defenders appealed for a foul, but the referee preferred to interpret the incident as an example of Haaland's sheer strength and power.

Just before half-time we were awarded a soft penalty, after the VAR muppets adjudged that a trip on Bernardo Silva was worth another look. To the naked eye, the offence seemed far less obvious than two previous incidents which hadn't been reviewed, but this was par for the course. Haaland's finish from the spot was composed and emphatic, drilling the ball low to Sánchez's left.

Expectations of another Etihad procession were realigned early in the second half, when the dangerous Leandro Trossard struck with a fierce low shot, and for the next 20 minutes or so the game was in the balance as Brighton displayed the qualities which had won them so many admirers. But the decisive moment came with 15 minutes remaining.

Kevin De Bruyne had as usual been racking up the assists as well as being involved in so many other goals – in the derby he'd had a hand in four of the six. What had been missing was goals, with just one so far, but here he stepped up to the mark at a vital time, a classic 25-yarder arrowing into the top corner. The goal put an end to Brighton's spirited attempts to fight back, but the fact that they'd enjoyed 52 per cent of possession – the first side to boss the ball against us all season – illustrated what De Zerbi was trying to do, and their results would soon more accurately reflect their performances.

The following week, away at struggling Leicester, a turgid game saw City struggle to impose themselves against a side bereft of attacking ambition. The fact that Haaland was missing with a minor foot injury didn't help, but Leicester's ultra-deep 5-4-1 setup would have stifled most teams. The decisive moment came early in the second half, De Bruyne's free kick from fully 25 yards clearing the wall, then dipping to clip the underside of the bar before hitting the net. When it came to Kevin's goals so far this season, it was a case of quality over quantity – there'd only been three, but each was an absolute gem.

Next up were Marco Silva's Fulham, who after their promotion had defied expectations that they'd be lightweight relegation fodder, pleasing on the eye but with insufficient substance to survive in the big boys' league. Their opening-day draw with Liverpool had set the tone, and they'd built on it with some impressive results and performances. Even so, most of us expect this to be a relatively straightforward afternoon, especially given the absence of Aleksandar Mitrović. Sure enough, City dominate the ball and take the lead when Álvarez bursts through on to a perfectly weighted Gundo pass and thumps a ferocious drive in off the underside of the bar. It's a finish which again is decidedly Agüero-esque, as the young Argentine continues to impress. And it looks as though the recuperating Haaland will be able to stay resting on the bench.

Fulham have scarcely threatened until some sloppy defending sees Harry Wilson suddenly burst clear. As he moves into the area and prepares to shoot, João Cancelo comes across and barges him to the ground. It's an obvious penalty and, as Cancelo made no attempt to play the ball, a red card as well. There's plenty of derision from the stands, but it's not even debatable. The challenge was not just clumsy but utterly brainless. Pep generally finds it easy to forgive mistakes when the intention is good; forgiving thoughtless acts of stupidity is something he struggles with. Several players have found themselves out in the cold for a period after just a single bad decision has cost the team – Kyle Walker and Fabian Delph immediately spring to mind – and no one would be surprised if the same fate now befell Cancelo. As Pereira calmly slots the penalty home to equalise, Pep holds his head in his hands. An hour to play with a man down against a decent team in a game we have to win.

Fulham help by deciding not to chance their arm, and even with ten men we dominate possession and don't concede any chances of note. But we don't create a great deal either, and just after the hour mark Pep bows to the inevitable and brings Haaland off the bench. I suspect he didn't really want to, with the big man having been left there just in case of emergency. This is an emergency. The crowd are energised, and within minutes Erling finds the net, soaring to head home a perfect cross from De Bruyne, only for VAR to rule him offside.

As we move into added time it looks as though our increasingly frantic efforts will be in vain, and for sure you wouldn't want to be João Cancelo in the dressing room afterwards. Then, De Bruyne fastens on to a knockdown in the area and as he pirouettes he receives the slightest clip on his ankle from Antonee Robinson. It's enough for him to go to ground and Darren England points instantly to the spot. Soft, but the right decision. These days you hardly ever see penalties that aren't soft.

So once again into the spotlight steps Erling Haaland. He's three from three on spot-kicks so far, but none of them have been quite as important as this one. He goes through his usual routine before sprinting up and side-footing the ball to Leno's right. It's not absolutely in the corner but that proves to be a saving grace, as the ball passes beneath the keeper's body and into the net. The merits of keeping the ball on the ground have seldom been better illustrated – a foot in the air and Leno would have got something on it. As Haaland wheels away in delight he takes his shirt off and twirls it in the air – the afternoon's second Agüero-esque moment – as Pep fist-pumps with delight and the crowd exult.

The final whistle blows a few seconds later, prompting extraordinary scenes of celebration for a win over a mid-table side in the first third of the season. The players – and Pep – complete a full lap of honour with Haaland leading the way, as much with relief as joy. 'It was one of the most nervous moments of my life,' he said afterwards. 'When you go down to ten against 11 for 70 minutes, I don't think any team would do it as well as we did today, so all praise to all the guys who made it possible.' On *Match of the Day*, Gary Lineker was in agreement, suggesting that the Premier League might be a more even contest if we started every game with ten men. Come on, Gary, we're good, but we're not that good.

Pep's exuberance continues after the match. 'It was so exciting. After seven years, you always have doubts, "Do people still follow you, are they tired, are they annoyed in their jobs?" Many thousands of millions of meetings, training sessions and travel, but today you say, "Wow," you see they still want to do it, they are still alive and they make us so, so proud. The way they played today is the reason why I am a manager. It was one of the best experiences we've ever had here.'

Jonathan Northcroft in *The Times* was certainly impressed, observing, 'The quick, fluent and daring way City kept moving the ball even when a man down was a wonder: they had 72 per cent possession with 11 men, and 71 per cent possession with ten.' But there are two sides to this and, outstanding as we'd been, Fulham's timid approach when presented with a man advantage for such a long time certainly played into our hands. As Micky Gray told talkSPORT listeners, 'Fulham deserved everything they got from the game. Which was absolutely nothing.'

After Cancelo had trudged off the field, we expected him to head down the tunnel without making eye contact. Instead Pep took hold of him and engaged him in conversation. Afterwards, he confirmed the gist of what he'd said. 'João should let them score a goal.' If they score, they score, but Ederson's much better at one-on-ones than he is at saving penalties. We got away with it in the end, but we have to learn. Another incident like this in a more important game could cost us everything.

8

12 November 2022, Premier League:
City 1 Brentford 2

'They might be Man City but they're
humans and humans can lose games'

SO NOW we're just a week away from an enforced six-week break to accommodate the World Cup, and with no fewer than 16 of our squad – every senior player bar Haaland and Mahrez – due to participate, there's a natural fear that one or two of them may have their thoughts on Qatar.

Firstly we face a Carabao Cup tie at home to Chelsea, and we put out what you might call our Carabao Cup side – as do Chelsea. It's a tremendously entertaining game, City bossing possession but Chelsea having the better chances, and cup keeper Stefan Ortega really shines, with some excellent saves. His distribution is also impressive, and we now seem to have a backup keeper capable of challenging Ederson. City improve in the second half, not that they were bad in the first, and open the scoring with a 20-yard free kick from Mahrez. It didn't look to have the elevation to clear the wall, but replays show that Koulibaly simply couldn't be arsed to jump as the ball passed directly and narrowly above his head.

City struck again almost immediately with a goal which showed again what an asset Julián Álvarez is. Picking the ball up by the left touchline he pinged a superb diagonal pass over to Mahrez on the right. By the time Mahrez had cut inside and forced Mendy into a full-stretch low save, Álvarez was arriving in the six-yard box to tap the loose ball home.

There was time for more excellence from Ortega to maintain our breathing space, but undoubtedly the night's star turn had been Jack Grealish, positive from the start, running at, committing and beating defenders and generally enjoying himself. He also got a few decent shots away, forcing Mendy into a couple of top saves. Admittedly it was a lower-profile match, but this demonstration that he had the confidence to take a game by the scruff of the neck was certainly encouraging.

Another player to enjoy himself was Kalvin Phillips, back from injury and being afforded 45 minutes as a replacement for Rodri. More importantly, it allowed Phillips to prove himself fit ahead of Gareth Southgate's squad announcement for Qatar, and Southgate duly remained loyal to the man who'd performed so well for him at the previous major international tournament. Let's hope Kalvin can get back to form and fitness and come back as the player we thought we were getting.

So, the season's first phase finishes with a home game against Brentford. In a way, it's the worst possible fixture, with Thomas Frank's side having only a handful of players named in the competing World Cup squads. And after an impressive start to life in the Premier League, they've shown no sign of second-season syndrome thus far. They may be light on household names over at the bus stop in Hounslow, but they're not a side to be taken lightly.

Even before the match, Pep expresses concern about the players' mindset. 'If you got an injury against Brentford it's not going to change anything in terms of winning the Premier League or not. But the players may say, "I'm going to miss the World Cup because of it. What am I going to do? How am I going to play?" I have to tell the guys to be focused. We play Saturday, then on Sunday they have got to be with the national team so I'm pretty sure that this will be a little bit in the players' minds. It's normal. I would be the same.' But what you certainly don't need against a side as committed and well-organised as this one is any lack of focus.

It's immediately evident that this is going to be a very tricky afternoon. Brentford are the more dangerous side from the start, and a smart interchange sees them put Onyeka through on Ederson. John Stones is in close pursuit but pulls out of a challenge, the lesson of last week evidently well-cemented, and Ederson spreads himself to make an excellent save. But the lesson of how dangerous Brentford can be on the break isn't quite so well learned. When KDB gifts the ball to Rico Henry, his surge down the left ends with Toney being presented with a great chance. You'd put your house on him to score – and so would he – but he allows Ederson to make another top stop.

They're a big old side, so an important priority is to avoid conceding set pieces. When Cancelo – back in the team after serving his suspension in the Carabao Cup tie in which he wouldn't have played anyway – who makes these rules, honestly – gives away a free kick in his own half, you'd expect it to be an innocuous situation. But Briars lumps it forward, Mee outjumps Akanji to flick it on and Toney gets above Laporte to loop it over Ederson. It's a proper old-school Wimbledon-type goal, but on the balance of play so far it's fully deserved.

It's been an uncomfortable watch, but City gradually establish territorial dominance without testing Raya, although there's a frenzied period of play which sees no fewer than four penalty appeals within a couple of minutes. After a protracted VAR review, Rico Henry's clear handball is deemed to be literally two inches outside the area, and from the resulting free kick there are three further appeals within ten seconds, none of them remotely convincing. But at least it gets the crowd fired up. Finally, in added time, Foden drives a sweet, angled half-volley high into the net, and the chat at the interval is all about City imposing ourselves after the break. But just as we seek to build some second half momentum, Laporte gets an elbow in the head and there's a seven-minute delay while he's bandaged up, draining energy from the crowd.

City do have some chances but Brentford have just as many, and probably the more clear-cut ones, with Ederson being called into action more than in any other game this season. And then, in the eighth minute of added time, De Bruyne pulls out of a tackle close to the Brentford area, where others would have taken a yellow for the team, and the break is on. Three of their players sprint forward and the move ends with a ball across the face of the goal being tapped home by Toney. As we throw bodies forward in search of an equaliser, Brentford break once again and Toney slides the ball past Ederson only to find Kev on hand to clear off the line. But the game's up. Toney has had five great chances, and we just haven't been able to cope with him. Far from being demoralised by his omission from Southgate's squad, Toney's been hell-bent on proving him wrong, the biggest handful we've encountered at the Etihad since Harry Kane last season. 'They might be Man City but they're humans and humans can lose games,' he says. Indeed they can.

An understandably thrilled Thomas Frank hails the result as the best in Brentford's history. Pep has no argument with the outcome, lamenting that we just couldn't cope with Toney, with his team-mates surrounding him to pick up knockdowns, flicks and second balls. There may have been Route One elements about their play – they would go on to register the highest proportion of long balls in the league throughout the season, almost a third – but once they got the ball on the ground they used it to great effect and with real quality. Defensively they were equally impressive, the first time all season Haaland had failed to register a shot on target, although much of the credit for that was down to them also restricting De Bruyne.

It feels like all the good work against Fulham has been undone, but there's no question that Brentford deserved it. Pep seems quite calm in the press conference, maybe also relishing the chance to take a break, and offers no excuses, no complaints about the marginal penalty call not given – 'that would be disrespectful to Brentford' – and refuting any suggestion that the World Cup was playing on players' minds.

It's certainly not the best way to go into a six-week break, and when Arsenal beat Wolves later in the day they're five points ahead and there are teams behind us breathing down our necks. But we've played just 14 matches, barely a third of the season. When the Premier League resumes it'll be like a completely new season. We haven't played Arsenal at all yet, so arithmetically the title is still in our hands. No cause for alarm. We're still well in the frame, still alive in every other competition and no one puts together late season winning runs quite like we do. There have been some disappointments but far more highlights, and moments of individual brilliance that we'll never forget. And when we come back this bad day at the office will be long forgotten.

9

28 December 2022, Premier League:
Leeds United 1 City 3

*'I could have scored a couple
more but that's life'*

EVERY PREMIER League manager watches the World
Cup praying that none of their players get injured, and
probably hoping that the countries they're representing get
knocked out in the quarter-final stage at the latest, to allow
a decent period of rest and chance to reacclimatise before
the proper football recommences. But when you've got 16
players competing there are bound to be some whose teams
don't comply with your wishes.

It turns out to be a World Cup of surprises, the main one
being that there's lots of exciting and enterprising football.
A most welcome development is that for the first time ever,
referees add on time which accurately reflects the time
wasted, and there are plenty of instances where the added
time reaches double figures.

The biggest individual disappointment among City's
representatives is Kevin De Bruyne, completely out of sorts
in each of Belgium's three matches. And he doesn't get the
chance to play himself into form, as his team suffer a shock

elimination, falling at the group stage. The revelation from City's perspective is Julián Álvarez, who features in all of Argentina's games, starts the last five, scores four goals and proves to be a pivotal player in their triumphant tournament. His influence extends as far as the final against France, with some outstanding play helping to set up his team's second goal. Argentina looked to be strolling to victory but a late French comeback sparked a dramatic period of extra time, as thrilling a finale as the competition has ever witnessed. Eventually Argentina prevailed, becoming world champions by the grossly unsatisfactory means of a penalty shoot-out, simultaneously delivering a fairytale ending to Lionel Messi's international career and heartbreak for the superlative Kylian Mbappé, whose hat-trick proved to be of no avail. Mbappé's feat at least provoked much the best commentary line of the competition, with Ally McCoist observing that he'd scored 'the first World Cup Final hat-trick where all three goals were over the line'.

Meanwhile, Erling's been a bit bored. 'I've been at home, a bit mad that I've not been at the World Cup. I recharged my batteries. Watching other people score to win games at the World Cup triggered, motivated and irritated me. I'm more hungry and more ready than ever.' Qatar's loss could be City's gain.

And yet City's biggest gain throughout their enforced hiatus came off the pitch, with the news that Pep Guardiola had extended his contract by a further two years. So, with Pep evidently being a man of his word and perhaps the manager in football history least likely to be sacked, he'll be here until 2025, making it nine years in total. His interviews don't tell us anything we didn't already know, Pep saying that the setup at City and the support he receives make it the ideal environment for him to shine. With the integration of Haaland still a work in progress and the small matter of the Champions League on the agenda, there's plenty to keep him fully motivated.

Incredibly, just four days after the World Cup Final, City are back in action. It's a fourth-round Carabao Cup tie against Liverpool, and both clubs put out sides as strong as can reasonably be expected. City's one absentee is Álvarez, still in Argentina enjoying protracted celebrations, which we can only hope will prove to be useful practice for what might be to come. Fortunately for City, we've got a decent alternative waiting in the wings, with Haaland itching to get back into action.

Within just ten seconds he gets a great chance to banish his frustrations, but his attempted lob over Kelleher flies way over the bar. He has to wait all of ten minutes before getting back in the groove, meeting De Bruyne's excellent cross with an improvised near-post finish. City squander other opportunities before Carvalho equalises from Liverpool's first attempt, and the hapless Núñez misses two great chances to put them ahead despite City's general dominance.

Within a minute of the restart our other senior World Cup absentee, Riyad Mahrez, delivers a wonderful finish, a typically featherlight first touch followed by an equally familiar cut inside and whipped left-footer into the far corner. It's a goal of sheer beauty but, even as the fans continue to savour it, Núñez surges to the other end and cuts the ball back for Salah to tap home an equaliser.

As usual, a Liverpool goal gets Jamie Carragher seriously overexcited on Sky Sports, as he claims that this game is streets ahead of the World Cup Final. He's only referring to the first 49 minutes of each, but the reality is that, certainly when at full strength, both these teams would beat both of the finalists, probably with something to spare. How many of the Argentinian side would get into City's strongest team? Fingers of one hand? Maybe just the fingers of one finger.

The tie is decided when another exquisite cross from De Bruyne is guided home by Nathan Aké, although City have a late escape when Núñez misses another sitter. It's been a thrilling match, the quality and intensity of which has surprised and delighted everyone who thought a low-key resumption of domestic football inevitable. The result is fair enough and, remarkably, our standout performer is De Bruyne, unrecognisable from the player in Qatar but hearteningly familiar to everyone here at the Etihad. Pep's delighted with him, and interestingly says that the players who went to Qatar are in much better rhythm than those who stayed behind. If this is what Haaland and Mahrez are like when they're out of rhythm, then God help the opposition when they find it.

And the next opposition, as the Premier League resumes, will be Leeds United at Elland Road. 'It won't be a friendly game,' offers Pep with some understatement, as he prepares his side for the hostile atmosphere and uncompromising physical approach of Jesse Marsch's team. And it'll be a special night for Erling Haaland, not only returning to the city of his birth but also being reunited with his manager from the Salzburg years.

It should also have been a special night for Kalvin Phillips, whose move from Leeds has thus far been not so much a damp squib as a complete non-event, but he won't be featuring at Elland Road. On being asked why, Pep states, matter-of-factly, 'He's not injured, he's overweight. He didn't arrive in the condition to do training sessions. It's a private conversation with Kalvin.' This really doesn't bode well for Phillips's future prospects at the Etihad.

City are excellent from the start, and Haaland again has a first-minute opportunity, but his attempted chip over Meslier is palmed to safety by the young keeper. Haaland is again denied later in the half but much the easiest chances fall to Jack Grealish. He's never been renowned as a goalscorer but his efforts here are abysmal, first reaching for a cross with his right foot when his left would have been a far better option, then embarrassingly scooping a simple opportunity over the bar. At least he's not the only culprit, as Haaland, Gündoğan and Mahrez also spurn chances you'd expect them to take. But just as a half of total dominance looks like ending goalless we at last take the lead, when Rodri slots home after Meslier can only parry Riyad's shot into his path. It's a lead which has been long overdue, as Leeds have barely laid a glove on us.

The second half provides what might prove to be a watershed moment. A sloppy pass out of defence is intercepted by Grealish, who sprints forward with Haaland alongside him. As Meslier comes out, Jack slides the ball across to give Erling a tap-in. As the ball hits the net, Grealish runs away to the corner, fists clenched as though he himself had scored the goal. His relief at having made a goal contribution means so much to him, and a few minutes later he racks up another, this time with a smart first-time cut-back for Haaland to fire through Meslier's hands and make the game safe.

Leeds grab a late consolation when Pascal Struijk heads home from a corner, prompting disproportionate celebrations from the intensely irritating Marsch, and they almost set up a nervy finish when Gnonto puts a great chance wide, but they end up well beaten and City can take real satisfaction from the way they've got back into things after the long break. It's Haaland who'll be making the headlines again but, after his woeful first-half misses, Grealish has racked up a couple of assists. How much better will he feel after that?

And tonight Pep's been impressed with the whole team. 'They are in 25-degree heat in Qatar, then you come here with this weather, to Elland Road against the most intense team in the Premier League. You don't know how you're going to react. But they reacted really well.' And no one reacted better than Kevin De Bruyne, excellent throughout, the memory of his mysteriously substandard World Cup seemingly already behind him. 'Sometimes to find the right fire inside of himself, he has to be a little bit grumpy to play his best. When this happens, what a player,' says Pep.

For Erling, it was another day, another couple of goals. 'We have to hunt Arsenal. I could have scored a couple more but that's life and I have to train more. At Salzburg it was hard for me when I missed chances but I'm getting older, more mature and getting a bit better at handling these situations. Of course, it's hard and you have to think about the next chance because you cannot do anything about the past.'

Pep surprised reporters by saying that, despite his nice rest in front of the telly, Erling wasn't yet back at full throttle. 'I think he is still not at his best like at the beginning of the season, but the injury he had against Dortmund affected him for a long period. I am still more than satisfied but I had the feeling in the first part of the season he was sharper.' As for Kalvin Phillips's physical condition, 'Yeah, he has a perfect body, really — so sexy.'

Three days later, Everton come to the Etihad with manager Frank Lampard under pressure. It's a fractious game from the outset, with the visitors looking to run the clock down from the first minute and Haaland taking early exception to a challenge from Ben Godfrey. Midway through the half, excellent play from Mahrez allows Haaland to squeeze home the opener. The shape of the game doesn't change at all, Everton still defending deep, essentially with a back eight, and City striving for a further breakthrough.

Despite having scored and most unusually celebrated with an aggressive gesture towards the Everton defenders, Haaland is still visibly wound up and after John Stones heads against the outside of the post, the striker pursues the ball with gusto and clatters into Mykolenko with a sliding tackle. He gets a yellow card, and maybe isn't too far away from the red which several Everton players are demanding.

Half-time comes, giving the players a chance to calm down, and shortly into the second half comes a long unscheduled delay as the linesman's malfunctioning equipment takes an age to repair. City struggle to regain any rhythm but Everton can't muster a threat until a rare mistake from Rodri allows Demarai Gray to make a run to the corner of the area. With Akanji distracted by Mykolenko's overlapping run, Gray has time and space to look up, and his dipping curler clears Ederson to find the top corner. It's a phenomenal strike, if totally unmerited on the balance of play, and strengthens Everton's determination not to concede again. The final 15 minutes are played out exclusively in and around the Everton area but despite numerous scrambles the visitors hold on for their point. Lampard's cynical tactics have hardly endeared him to City fans and his post-match interview further tarnishes his reputation, claiming that his side got what they deserved for 'staying in the game'. But there's karma in the offing, as Everton fail to build on their ill-gotten point and Lampard is dismissed three weeks later.

When Arsenal win impressively at Brighton, they find themselves seven points clear and for the first time some pundits are suggesting that they could actually go all the way. There's no need to panic yet, but City's margin for error is getting ever smaller.

10

5 January 2023, Premier League: Chelsea 0 City 1

'I didn't realise how hard it is to adapt to a different team'

AFTER SUCH a disappointing result, the new year began with a visit to Stamford Bridge, usually one of the season's toughest assignments. But this wasn't anything like a usual season for Chelsea, now under the ownership of megabucks American Todd Boehly, a man whose initial utterances gave the overwhelming impression that he had absolutely no idea what he was doing.

Having sacked Thomas Tuchel less than a month into the season, Boehly had replaced him with Brighton's Graham Potter, whose achievements on the south coast certainly merited a crack at one of the big boys. It was expected that Potter, already having years of Premier League experience under his belt, would bring about an immediate upturn in fortunes but the reverse proved to be the case, as the club's basket-case scattergun transfer policy left had left him with an absurd amount of experienced internationals to select from.

There's a still frequently touted myth that City have a huge depth of squad but the reality is that there are just 16 senior outfield players vying for the ten starting spots in the most important games. That would become 17 if Phillips ever gets up to speed. The squad is topped up by academy products such as Lewis and Palmer and younger transferees such as Sergio Gómez, essentially bought as a player for the future. Compared with Chelsea's mammoth accumulation of talent, much of which might as well spend its weekends going shopping at Harrods as there isn't even room for it on the bench, we're down to the bare bones.

This season, Chelsea have been awash with underperformers, not least their summer acquisition from City, Raheem Sterling. Not that City fans would necessarily have been surprised, as despite his undeniable contribution to our successes, Sterling had divided opinion ever since he arrived in 2015.

I go back to 1967. Never in all that time have we had a player who provided so many 'how the fuck did he miss that' moments. His pace often enabled him to burst through one-on-one with the keeper and in the early days fans would be out of their seats in anticipation as he prepared to pull the trigger. After a while, most of us couldn't be bothered to even watch, never mind stand up, knowing that the chance would end up with him being overcome by indecision and falling over his own feet or with the ball being lamped over the bar as he simply panicked and hoped for the best.

Of course there were some great, positive memories as well, like the 2017 added-time winner against Southampton, a fabulous curler from the edge of the box which retained City's winning streak and sent the watching Benjamin Mendy on an equally memorable crutch-assisted hop of delight down the touchline. And his final appearance for City, on as a substitute on that famous afternoon against Villa, saw him trigger the comeback, shifting the ball to get a yard of space close to the corner flag before crossing perfectly for Gundo to nod home.

We live in a stats-obsessed world and with 131 career goals for City – fifth in the post-war list and a tally amassed over just seven seasons – it should be a shoo-in for Sterling to be regarded as a true City great. And yet he's looked back on with a sense of ambivalence. There's so much to admire about him and like most City fans I really tried to love him, but it's hard to think of a less aesthetically pleasing, more exasperating player.

His frustration at no longer being a regular starter boiled over, but when you're competing against Bernardo, Riyad and Phil, you've got to be playing at your best to hold down a regular place – or even an occasional place. And for most of last season Raz wasn't, although he evidently struggled to see it that way. 'Everyone wants to feel wanted. When you play your heart out, sacrifice some of your kids' birthdays, and then get treated in a certain way, it's disappointing. At the time I was fuming, raging, and it didn't make sense to fight a battle you couldn't win. It was the right time to move on.' And City certainly weren't going to stand in his way.

You always fear that you've made a mistake when you sell a player to a rival, but so far there'd been little sign of Sterling recapturing any kind of form. Even so, there can't have been a City fan who didn't fear the worst when he took to the field against us at Stamford Bridge. Sadly his chance to remind us of what we'd lost lasted just five minutes before he was struck down by injury. It was cruel luck on Raz, yet it epitomised a downturn in his career which he'll do well to recover from.

Chelsea, low on confidence and with other key players also unavailable, were surely there for the taking but City were again sluggish, as if suffering a hangover from

Everton's New Year's Eve smash-and-grab, and it was the home side who came closest to scoring in the first half when Chukwuemeka's low shot came back off a post.

The way we'd played against Liverpool and Leeds had given the impression that we'd clicked instantly back into the groove after the World Cup, but now everything seemed to be a struggle. Unusually, if not uniquely, Pep's dissatisfaction at half-time manifested itself by way of two tactical substitutions, Akanji for Walker and young Rico Lewis for Cancelo. There was an improvement in our midfield control, Lewis slotting in effortlessly and helping us to maintain sequences of possession, but still little goal threat, although Nathan Aké evened up the hit the woodwork scoreboard when his header from De Bruyne's free kick struck the outside of the post.

Despite the improvement, Guardiola sensed that further changes were needed, next hooking Foden and Bernardo and bringing on Grealish and Mahrez. This was positively weird behaviour, four tactical substitutions by the hour mark. Had it ever happened before, other than when City had already put the game to bed? Maybe it was Pep's new year's resolution.

Whatever, it worked as well as any substitution he'd ever made; within just three minutes the two new entrants combined to give City the lead. De Bruyne fed Grealish on the left and, rather than taking the usual couple of touches, Jack immediately slid a lovely ball across the face of goal and in at the far post came Mahrez to slide the ball home. And maybe that's why they call Pep a genius.

City held on to what they had in relative comfort, apart from a foray down the left in the final seconds when young Lewis Hall blazed over the bar, but overall it had been a 'take the points and move on' sort of performance. Still, Pep seemed happy enough. 'The people believe in November we are already champions and this is impossible. Arsenal, United, the other teams don't have this pressure. After four Premier Leagues in five years it's not easy to push them again and that's why I'm satisfied – right now we are still there.'

Writing in *The Guardian*, Barney Ronay picked up colourfully on the familiar theme of Pep's efforts to integrate Haaland into the team. 'By the end City did look like a fluent attacking force, with Haaland finding a way to link and move with City's flank players. It is still a learning process. For six years the City story has been based around those overloads in attack, the extra man, the extra angles. This sleeker version is new for everyone. Here we have a team with ten Pep-issue parts, and one bolt-on goal-hammer. Haaland is a killer. Is a killer always what you want? This is a major shift for everyone else in this team. Victory here, with Haaland just another shoulder to the wheel, felt like another step towards solving this thing.'

It was another tangible contribution from Grealish, his third assist in three games, and he was refreshingly open about his struggles so far. 'When I came here it was so much more difficult than I thought. In my head I thought I was going to the team sitting top of the league and I was going to get so many goals and assists and obviously that didn't happen. A lot of teams tend to sit in against us and that wasn't the case at Villa. I didn't realise how hard it is to adapt to a different team and manager.'

But even when things weren't going well there was a sense that the media in general were willing him to succeed rather than rushing to brand him a '£100m flop'. There was evidently something about him that people liked. And Pep had always been supportive, saying, 'Grealish's body language is exceptional if he plays or doesn't play – these type of guys always play good.'

Pep also praised the contribution made by our newest discovery. 'In the first half everything was sloppy, we had no rhythm – but we got better when Rico came in. He has the ability and talent to make our game better. Most of the players play good, but he has the ability to play good but make the others play better. As a midfield player that talent is extraordinary.' This was high praise indeed, and the travelling fans seemed already to have taken Lewis to their hearts, chants of 'Rico! Rico!' ringing out after the final whistle.

With Arsenal having been held at home by a doggedly resilient Newcastle side, the gap at the top returned to a more manageable five points. With even a minor slip by the Gunners being taken by some as an indication that a decline was about to set in, the general consensus remained that City would soon launch one of those long winning runs and blow the north London pretenders away. Further evidence in support of City's prospects came with the demeanour of Arteta, whose manic behaviour towards the end of the Newcastle game suggested a man seriously feeling the pressure. We weren't even at the halfway stage of the season, yet frequently he was getting into a proper lather, hardly conducive to keeping his players calm under pressure. Equally, however, it was indicative of a mentality that the frequently cited target for Arsenal of a top-four finish was nonsense. This was a man going for gold in the marathon, but blowing a gasket halfway through the race wasn't going to help.

11

14 January 2023, Premier League: Manchester United 2 City 1

'It is what it is. But we know exactly where we play'

CITY'S RECORD under Pep in the Carabao Cup had been almost exemplary, testament to his desire to win every competition we enter. Our sequence of four successive Wembley wins was brought to an end by West Ham in a fourth-round penalty shoot-out a year ago, but the last occasion we lost in regulation time – the only time under Pep – was way back in 2016. And we certainly looked good for another strong showing this season as, having already seen off Chelsea and Liverpool, we faced what looked like a rather less demanding task in the quarter-final, with a trip to struggling Southampton.

As usual we fielded a strong side, with a fistful of first-team regulars on the bench in case things weren't going as planned. And they certainly didn't. Giving the lie that the most effective way to succeed against City was to sit deep, frustrate and counterattack, Southampton pressed aggressively from the start, and City coughed up mistake after mistake. Usually so patient and effective at playing through the press, it was an almost unrecognisable performance. Southampton fully merited the lead given to them by Sékou Mara, a sweet finish after Sergio Gómez had given the ball away, and they quickly doubled it with a sublime 30-yard chip from Moussa Djenepo, even if Ortega's positioning made the option particularly inviting.

Pep continued his newfound liking for half-time changes, with De Bruyne, Aké and Akanji all joining the fray, though the fact that Kalvin Phillips went on to last until just after the hour mark was more a testament to a desire to give Rodri a rest rather than reflecting any kind of satisfaction with the performance of the former Leeds man. His lack of match action was a mitigating factor, but he was way off the pace and frankly looked more like the sort of player City would have signed back in the dark, down-among-the-dead-men days of the late 1990s. It seemed inconceivable that an established England player, who'd also been so consistently excellent for Leeds, could perform so wretchedly. It had to be down to a lack of match fitness but as we moved towards the part of the season where every match is crucial, where was he going to get it?

The plan to rest the big guns ahead of the derby was further compromised when Haaland also came on, but he too had little impact as City succumbed meekly to a dismal defeat in what was one of the worst performances of the whole Guardiola regime. With not a single attempt on target, City's exit was thoroughly merited, as Pep openly conceded. 'The best team won. We had a bad night. I had the feeling today, it doesn't matter the line-up, we would perform in this way. Don't ask me why, it's my experience. We were not here. If we perform in this way against United we will not have a chance.'

Club captain İlkay Gündoğan also alluded to the mentality of the players not being quite right. 'In the last two weeks, I feel like something was missing. At the moment, the performances, the desire, the hunger is maybe not as it was. We showed a lack of attitude, commitment and confidence and we know that we have to do better, we need to start working hard again, we need to be humble, because wins will not come to us automatically. We need to deserve them.'

Hunger and desire have always been a given for Pep teams, so what had brought this on? Was it the impact of the World Cup? The tournament had ultimately ended in disappointment for everyone but Álvarez, and usually the players have a few weeks to get it out of their systems before they start thinking about club football again. This year, they'd been straight back to it, with no time to refocus. But whatever the reason, it was hard to imagine a lack of desire for the next match, away at Old Trafford.

* * *

City's recent record at the Theatre of Hate had been outstanding. We'd won on four of our last six league visits, with a couple of Carabao Cup victories thrown in for good measure. It was the ideal fixture to get ourselves out of this indifferent phase. United had put together a strong run of results and would be fully motivated to show how far they'd come since their drubbing at the Etihad. But for City, that provided even greater incentive to put them back in their box.

The match follows the expected pattern, City enjoying the bulk of possession but United always primed for the counterattack. We know this is what they do, but we're still making the kind of individual mistakes that give them opportunities. They have the better of relatively few first-half chances, largely emanating from breaks down the left when we turn over possession with Kyle Walker pushed up and out of position. We're especially grateful for Rashford's heavy touch as he bears down on goal, and also for Akanji's awareness, getting back to cover after Ederson's ill-judged excursion from his area allows Martial to break free.

We've created so little, but the second half immediately has a different feel. We quickly get on top, and it's like a rerun of the game at Stamford Bridge. We're pinning them back, hunting the ball voraciously whenever we lose it, and knocking at the door. Just after the hour Foden makes way for Grealish, who immediately looks not just lively but also threatening. And incredibly, just as at Stamford Bridge, he makes an immediate impact. De Bruyne finds space down the right and stands up an inviting ball. With Haaland as ever taking up defensive attention, Grealish steals unmarked into the centre of the area and plants a header past De Gea. Once again, three minutes have elapsed since Jack entered the fray. Come on, Pep, now you're just showing off.

With 20 minutes left, the increasingly ineffective Eriksen is replaced by Alejandro Garnacho, the newest in a long line of New George Bests the vast majority of whom end up playing lower-league football as the stark realisation dawns that being a flashy selfish twat isn't necessarily the way to hold down a career in a side looking to challenge for major honours. Generally I'm always happy to see United acquire another player of this ilk, and put up with the hype that inevitably results after they pull off a few nutmegs or execute a couple of step-overs or even score a goal or two. Antony and Sancho are the latest showboating dilettantes who look destined to achieve precious little, but this kid does look like he has something about him, and he's been influential in several of their recent late wins.

We're still in control, and when Rashford speeds on to a through pass our back line has pushed up in exemplary fashion to catch him well offside. There's no immediate flag from the linesman, the norm these days, and Rashford continues his run. Suddenly, up alongside him is Bruno Fernandes, who's sprinted forward. As the two of them reach the edge of the area, they both look primed to shoot, but it's Fernandes who slots the ball past Ederson, only to have his celebrations cut short by the immediate sight of the linesman's flag. There are protests from Fernandes – as sure as night follows day – and initially I'm not worried as Rashford was obviously offside and had clearly been in possession of the ball. But he hadn't actually touched it.

United are trying to make a case for saying he wasn't interfering with play – or whatever this season's terminology is – even though he basically shepherded the ball while waiting for Fernandes to arrive. But could any City players have got to it if he hadn't been there? Did he distract Ederson as the keeper attempted to save the shot? After a delay while the referee is advised by the VAR team, he trots over for a conversation with the linesman and I've got a sinking feeling. They've found a way to allow the goal.

On BT Sport, Peter Walton tells viewers, in that painfully familiar bumbling style of his, that the decision is the correct one, which the more discerning take as cast-iron confirmation that the goal should have been disallowed. He pins it on the fact that City defenders weren't directly affected by Rashford's run and technically you can make a case for saying that's true. Akanji directly pursues Rashford but, if Saint Marcus hadn't been there, he would surely have changed the angle of his run to get closer to Fernandes instead. He wouldn't necessarily have reached him, but may at least have done enough to distract him. And at the point Fernandes hit the shot, Rashford was so close to him that he had to check his stride to stop the two of them getting into a tangle. Ederson was faced with two United players bearing down on him, either of whom could have struck the ball. It was difficult to understand how that couldn't have been a distraction.

The general consensus was that to allow the goal to stand was a ridiculous decision, but now it's been made we need to put it to the back of our minds. Instead, we're visibly rocked, as a crowd renowned for being less noisy than the members' area at the real Old Trafford during a County Championship match bursts into life. Just four minutes later, Garnacho breaks free down the left, and eventually gets a yard on Aké to fizz a low ball across the six-yard box. Rashford gets ahead of the dozing Akanji and prods the ball under Ederson to put United ahead and you already sense that it's game over. They see out time in relative comfort and, in the time-honoured tradition of fans who've witnessed their heroes pull off a shock giant-killing, the place is bouncing, which given the state of the stadium could have serious health and safety ramifications for everyone inside it.

We may not like it – indeed we certainly don't – but despite their often laboured and uninspiring performances and looking a distinctly ordinary outfit, United are now just a single point behind us. The old cliche is that if you can win when playing badly then it's the sign of a good side, although when you do it repeatedly most of us prefer to interpret it as the sign of a lucky one. But this doesn't stop the murmurs about United being in the title race. You cannot be serious. But some of them are.

Under the circumstances, Pep is extraordinarily gracious in defeat and in particular points to the concession of the second goal so quickly after the first, suggesting a difficulty in putting it out of the players' minds. 'We have to improve after we concede a goal, to be more stable.' In effect he's saying that he's more upset about the second goal than the first, because that's the one where we should have done better. There are things that you can't control, and the decision to allow Fernandes's goal is one of them. He says, 'It is what it is. But we know exactly where we play. For the referee it is not easy.' For 'This is Anfield' read 'This is Old Trafford'. We've got some way to go before 'This is the Etihad' carries the same weight.

There are of course those who insist that it was a perfectly legitimate goal. You'll never guess where they used to play. Rio Ferdinand's view was, 'Rashford doesn't impact any of the defenders' running strides, patterns or positions. It is intelligent from him and Fernandes. I don't feel any of the defenders can influence any of it,' while erstwhile team-mate Paul Scholes claimed, 'He's interfering with nobody. It is good communication and a great finish.' One wonders how they would have reacted had the goal been awarded against them, though that, of course, could only ever be a hypothetical question.

Referees' supremo Howard Webb announces that the laws will be changed to ensure that goals like United's first will never again be allowed to stand. If anything, that makes us feel even worse. Keith Hackett, Webb's predecessor, is even more unequivocal. 'The authorities will put up a defence for referee Stuart Attwell and argue that Rashford did not interfere with play, but it is rubbish. This is a decision you cannot justify. They will argue that he has to touch the ball to be active. The law is awful and requires a complete rewrite.'

The Guardian's Will Unwin reflected the generally held view. 'Awarding the goal made little sense considering the involvement of Rashford. It turned the tide of the match in United's favour and could have a heavy impact on the title race.' Indeed it could, and all we can do is suck it up and move on.

Ten Hag naturally praises the fight and spirit of his players, but at least acknowledges that he 'wouldn't be happy if we conceded a goal like this'. Meanwhile Fernandes, the man who scored the goal, makes an interesting claim about team spirit and player attitude. 'Some time ago you could see some of us looking a little bit for ourselves, but now you see a proper team that works hard for each other, and it pays.'

We'll come back to that one.

12

18 January 2023, Premier League: City 4 Tottenham 2

'I don't want to be a happy flower. I want to beat Arsenal'

CITY ARE left to lick their wounds and harbour a sense of bitter injustice after the Old Trafford defeat, but Pep's real concern remained the team's reaction after the first United goal. The momentum shift made a second seem almost inevitable, bringing back memories of that still excruciatingly painful night at the Bernabéu. Setbacks happen, and no one knows, or reminds his players, more than Pep that the secret to winning these tight matches is, as he's so fond of saying, 'how you react in the bad moments'.

Although Pep claimed to be generally satisfied with the performance at Old Trafford, the fluency we'd seen so often in the early part of the season had, for now, gone missing. Despite the encouraging start immediately after the World Cup, City haven't hit the straps at all in the new year. With Arsenal now a full eight points clear – and United and others breathing down our necks – any further slips would put us in a position where even we might be unable to recover.

The expectation was that City would take out their frustrations in the next game, at home to Spurs. Two straight defeats were rare enough, but failing to win for a third successive time would almost constitute a crisis. At least there should be little chance of complacency, as Spurs had done the double over City the previous season, their opening-day win at the Tottenham Hotspur Stadium followed up by a dramatic 3-2 victory at the Etihad, thanks primarily to Harry Kane's stellar performance.

There are changes to the team sheet, with the hitherto highly impressive Rico Lewis getting a start, Grealish being rewarded for his recent encouraging cameos from the bench and Álvarez and Haaland playing in tandem. The most notable exclusion is Kev; the most noteworthy inclusion is Rico. It's a huge statement from Pep to start him in a game of such importance. Equally, it sends a message to the omitted Walker and Cancelo, both left on the bench, that they can't take their places for granted. Evidently, when Pep was so lavish in his praise of the youngster, he really meant it.

Spurs themselves were struggling, with Antonio Conte living up to his 'Mourinho Lite' reputation by employing stiflingly negative and unadventurous tactics, particularly in the first half of games. And it's clear early on that a core part of their approach tonight will be to intimidate Rico Lewis by, in layman's terms, kicking the shit out of him. Taking up that increasingly familiar role as an extra midfielder, Lewis is a core part of our build-up play, but several times finds himself clattered to the deck. He seems totally unfazed, just picking himself up, constantly making himself available to receive the ball and using it calmly and accurately, even firing in a couple of decent long-range efforts. There's nothing wrong with this boy's temperament and what again comes through is the total confidence shown in him by his team-mates, unhesitatingly playing the ball to him even in congested areas. The home fans are getting agitated though, not just by Tottenham's blatant targeting of the youngster but also by referee Simon Hooper's reluctance to bring out his yellow card.

As half-time approaches, City fashion their best chance so far, but despite a towering leap Haaland can't keep his header down, with Lloris in no man's land. Just a minute later, the ball's at the other end and Ederson unwisely and inaccurately plays it out towards Rodri on the edge of the area. Rodri has Bentancur snapping at his heels, and the ball gets nicked away to the oncoming Kulusevski, who calmly places it past the keeper. It's a bad mistake from Ederson, but given his heavy involvement in City's build-up play and the necessity to take risks in order to make progress, it's remarkable that it hasn't happened more often.

Just a minute later, Kane bursts through an unusually weak Rodri challenge on the right and drills the ball across goal. Ederson can only parry it into the air and Davinson Sánchez nods it into the vacant net. From nowhere, Spurs are two goals up – City once again conceding twice in quick succession – and the half-time whistle blows with the crowd barely able to take in what they've just witnessed. As the players leave the pitch, there's the rare sound of jeering, which will be referred to a lot in post-match interviews and analysis. It's taken by most to be directed at the team but from where I'm sitting, on the same side as the players' tunnel, most if not all of it is directed at the referee, with the noise intensifying as he approaches the tunnel. We've not played badly, it's just been a typical struggle to break down a well-organised and disciplined team, and Spurs have got a bonus they neither expected nor merited. But after the reverses at Southampton and Old Trafford, the talk in the concourses is, 'Are the wheels coming off?'

No half-time changes this time, as the players return for the most important 45 minutes of the season so far. Fail to turn this around, and Arsenal would have the chance to move 11 points clear. Even with half the season to go that's a hell of a lot to reel in.

Within eight minutes the game turns completely, the catalyst being the outstanding Mahrez. His cross from the right is only half-cleared by Lloris and Álvarez, sharp as a tack, crashes the loose ball home. And one goal is all it takes. We've come back so often from these situations that there's almost a sense of inevitability about what happens next, and it takes just a couple of minutes for us to draw level, Haaland nodding home from close range after being set up by Mahrez. Nothing unusual about that combination, although I'm struggling to remember whether Riyad has ever provided a headed assist before.

It looks like there's only one outcome, but Kulusevski suddenly breaks away in a rare counterattack, and cuts the ball back to Perišić, just eight yards out. A goal looks certain but Lewis manages to get in the way of the shot and it deflects off the post to safety. He's spent almost all of the game pushed up into midfield, but was true to his defensive roots here, and it's a vital intervention.

Despite their manager's reputation for defensive organisation, Spurs are a shambles at the back and when the ball is again played out towards Mahrez on the right, Perišić completely misses his attempted interception. Accelerating smoothly towards goal, Riyad drops his shoulder, goes outside Davies and lashes a low shot in at the near post. It's brilliant skill from the Algerian but another bad mistake from Lloris who, if you judged him purely by his performances at the Etihad over the years, would be lucky to get a game for Rochdale reserves.

Any remaining nerves are settled just as the added time board goes up, with another blunder – Clément Lenglet letting the ball pass by him – allowing Riyad a clear run towards Lloris. The outcome is never in doubt, the super-confident Mahrez classily clipping the ball over the falling keeper to seal yet another comeback victory. Riyad has been absolutely magnificent – he's in a real purple patch – but equally impressive has been Rico, already becoming a crowd favourite. From nowhere, we seem to have unearthed a *bona fide* squad member who can be trusted to play in big games.

Jamie Carragher was duly impressed, citing, 'Man City have got that thing now that Man Utd had when I was a player. You'd hear they were 2-0 down, but you didn't believe they'd get beaten. Man City have got that now.' On the touchline, Pep had been in super-animated mode as another epic comeback unfolded. Most expected him to be in buoyant mood afterwards, thrilled with another display of fighting spirit, but those first 45 minutes are still in his head. And doesn't he soon let everyone know it, firstly in his TV interviews and then in the press conference. 'I love my players so much and to win 4-2 against a fantastic team like Tottenham is good for us but I need to see desire and passion from the first minute to the last. We have to prepare better. I cannot deny how happy we are with the result but we are far away from the team that we were. Do you think this comeback will happen every time? It won't.

'We play because "my manager told me to do this and this" – but there is nothing from the stomach, the guts. We were lacking in guts, passion, fire, desire to win from minute one. I don't recognise my team. We were lucky, and if we don't change, sooner or later we are going to drop points. Rico Lewis suffers four fouls and, of course, no yellow card because it's Rico Lewis, and we don't react. Who defends him? No one. At Chelsea in the second half he arrived and changed the game. Why? Because "I want to live in this job and world. I want a better contract and to win Premier Leagues I have never won."

'We have an opponent in Arsenal who have the fire, almost two decades without winning the Premier League and every player knows they will make history, like we felt when we won the first Premier League and broke all the records and won back-to-back. I am explaining reality. Everything is so comfortable at City but opponents don't wait.'

He then turned to the fans. 'Our fans were silent for 45 minutes – I want my fans back! I want my fans here to support every corner and every action. Maybe it's the same as with our team, maybe we are so comfortable with winning four Premier Leagues in five years.

'They booed because we were losing, but not because we played bad. We played good. I want our fans to push us. Demand more. Say "come on guys". Show us more. We are a happy flowers team, all nice and good. I don't want to be a happy flower. I want to beat Arsenal. If we play that way Arsenal will destroy us. Do you think we are going to chase the gap to Arsenal the way we are playing? No way. Today we were lucky. We want to win something – but complaining, complaining, complaining – no chance we will win anything.'

It was an extraordinary and unprecedented outburst, and for sure well thought through. And it raised the question of who exactly is complaining? As long ago as 2017, Pep had said, 'You cannot create something when people who are not playing regularly are creating problems, Bad faces, bad behaviour from those guys ... when that happens, forget about it. You cannot stay if it happens.' So whose face has gone bad?

13

27 January 2023, FA Cup: City 1 Arsenal 0

'I think everyone in the locker room is happy for him, except maybe one person'

THE FA Cup. I love it. I've always loved it. It's probably a generational thing. With the huge increase in the number of matches shown on terrestrial TV in recent years, there's been a definite resurgence in the competition's popularity. And it's reflected in the fact that both main channels once again show the final live, just like in the good old days. The top clubs have started to take it seriously again, the big crowds are coming back. Fourth place might still be the more lucrative prize, but glory's back in fashion.

The third-round draw had paired City with Chelsea, who appeared to be not so much in a transitional phase as a meltdown. Just three days after our narrow league win at Stamford Bridge, the teams reconvened at the Etihad. When two sides of similar stature meet twice in such a small space of time, it often ends in a win apiece, and the second game's usually feisty, with grudges not yet forgotten carried over from the first meeting. But not here. Some of Chelsea's walking wounded had recovered, but their performance was pitifully weak as we cruised past them with barely a shred of resistance.

Mahrez launched a 25-yard free kick into the top corner, after which an inexplicable and initially undetected handball by Havertz led to a VAR-assisted penalty, duly squeezed home by Álvarez. More excellence from Riyad set up Foden to turn the ball home smartly before half-time, and the second half was more like a training exercise. With the travelling Chav Army calling for the return of the recently sacked Thomas Tuchel and indulging in ironic 'we've had a shot' chants when they finally mustered an effort on goal, City completed the scoring after Foden was barged over in the box, allowing Mahrez to bury the spot-kick.

Before the game had kicked off, City fans already knew that, if we won today, the fourth-round tie would be against Oxford United or Arsenal. Much as we'd have loved the Yellows to make it through, a top-of-the-table showdown was what everyone else wanted to see. And with a comfortable 3-0 win at the Kassam, Arsenal ensured that that was what we got.

The match was immediately moved to a Friday night for nationwide TV coverage and as kick-off approaches the expectation is that both teams will go strong. City certainly do, putting out what might reasonably be thought of as our strongest possible team, but Arteta makes several changes, leaving the likes of Ødegaard, Saliba, White and Martinelli on the bench. I'm really surprised. There's been nearly a full week since their previous game and there's a full week before the next one. This is nothing to do with disrespecting the FA Cup. It's the clearest possible statement that he thinks his side can win the league. Forget all the Sky Sports News talk of 'landing a psychological blow', the thing that matters most to Arteta is keeping players safe and well for the congested league schedule still to come.

Arteta's selection also changes the psychology of the game. If City win, Arsenal can say 'OK, but we didn't have our strongest side out, so we never expected to get a result,' whereas if we lose to a below-strength Arsenal side it'll be, 'We beat them even with half of our best team on the bench!' It's a surprising move from Arteta and for most observers a disappointing one – and to me a frightened and cowardly one, fearing the loss of self-belief if their full-strength side took a hiding.

The game itself also proves to be a bit of a disappointment, albeit ultimately helpful and instructive for City, as we struggle to overcome Arsenal's high press and man-for-man marking. It certainly appears as though Arteta's tactical approach has taken Guardiola a little by surprise. Ortega is reluctant to go long, frequently taking an age to find a free man, and the game has little flow.

Indeed, what flow there is in the first half comes mainly from the visitors, with Trossard, on his first start after moving from Brighton, particularly lively. A run down the left sees him cut the ball back for Tomiyasu to thrash in a fierce drive, well saved by Ortega, before the Belgian draws an even better save from City's cup keeper with a shot from the angle. A De Bruyne curler a foot past the post is the best City can muster in an underwhelming half. There's a puzzle to be solved here. But there's nothing that Pep likes more.

And the solution comes midway through the second half. Álvarez cleverly drops into space between the lines and when he receives the ball from Akanji, the Arsenal players are slow to react. He lines up a low shot, which skips past Turner but strikes the foot of the post. The rebound is collected by Grealish on the left and after some to-ing and fro-ing he finds a lovely angle to slip the ball into Nathan Aké. A precise, low, angled side-foot finds the far corner of Turner's net and we're in the lead.

Arsenal call for reinforcements and Nketiah almost gets on the end of a Martinelli cross with the goal gaping, but City hold on for the narrowest of victories. You wouldn't say we were lucky, but it was certainly a very even game, and could have gone either way. The most impressive part of City's performance was how well we controlled things after taking the lead. We hope we've learned more about them throughout the evening than they have about us. We shall see.

Pep admits that he was surprised by Arsenal's tactical approach, adapting in the second half by playing a few long balls up to Haaland. And why not? He's a six-foot-four powerhouse. So much of what he's done so far this season has surprised people; why not occasionally throw in a tactic which might be expected when you've got a big man up front?

It's been a great night for Nathan Aké, whose performance is highlighted in the media primarily because he scored the winner, but his all-round contribution, notably in dealing with Bukayo Saka, is what's really impressive, repeatedly winning their one-on-one duels. Aké has got stronger and stronger this season, the most consistent of our defenders, and is being rewarded with regular starts. The more he plays the better he gets, the better he gets, the more he plays. After the game, Pep is full of praise for his unlikely match-winner, offering up a cryptic comment which he almost shies away from making but he's just too late to stop himself. 'I think everyone in the locker room is happy for him … except maybe one person.'

It sets tongues wagging – especially after the 'complaining, complaining' remarks following the Spurs game – and speculation is rife. One of the most famous stories from Pep's Barcelona days, when he similarly had a bunch of players on the bench who would walk into most other teams – was to ask his staff to check their reactions when Barça scored a goal. The ones who didn't celebrate – preoccupied with themselves, sulking at not being in the starting 11, not happy for their team-mates – were noted, and by the beginning of the following season had been shipped out. One of the hardest things to do when it's a team game with so many individually brilliant parts is to instil a genuine team spirit, where everyone works for the collective good and supports each other. It's one of Pep's most fundamental principles. But it asks a lot of the players.

Looking at the line-ups, the likeliest contenders to have inherited Nicolas Anelka's 'Incredible Sulk' moniker appear to be Kyle Walker and João Cancelo, both left on the bench as Lewis and Aké were preferred. And within four days we get our answer as, completely out of the blue, the news emerges that Cancelo has joined Bayern Munich on loan, with an option to make the deal permanent. Cancelo has been such a vital part of our successes that it seems a strange move, especially with no time to bring in a replacement even if one were wanted. But Pep's 'no bad faces' mantra brooks no argument, and the sudden emergence of Lewis, a player with different attributes but the versatility to play a midfield role, makes it less of a risk.

Naturally, Cancelo's exit doesn't generate as many headlines as that of The Walking Ego from our neighbours a few weeks earlier and yet, as Richard Jolly observed in *The Independent*, it represented the bigger surprise. 'Ronaldo did not rank in Erik ten Hag's strongest team. Cancelo helped define Guardiola's side in the previous two seasons. He had seemed at the peak of his powers. City have let an outstanding footballer go for now without recouping a transfer fee or replacing him when they had not really replaced Oleksandr Zinchenko either.'

That's all correct, and it does leave us looking exposed on the left. But however bad Cancelo's face may have been, Pep isn't going to let him go without having a plan in mind.

14

5 February 2023, Premier League: Tottenham 1 City 0

'It's not the Manchester City of old'

CITY'S DRAMATIC home win over Spurs – and the even more dramatic interviews and press conference from Guardiola – seriously whetted the appetite for the next Premier League fixture, at home to Wolves. Much of the pre-match talk centred on Guardiola's rant and what the reaction from players and fans might be. The fans certainly got the message, with the noise and atmosphere noticeably ramped up from the start – indeed from well before the start.

This certainly wasn't the best version of Wolves seen here in recent years, with no real attacking threat and an over-robust approach to tackling which led to two yellow cards in the first 12 minutes. After a series of near-misses, City took the lead through an increasingly common combination. A switch to Mahrez in space on the right, the winger teasing the defence before slipping a ball into De Bruyne's run, then a perfect cross for the towering Haaland to head home at the far post.

In the second half, a silly trip on Mahrez brought a penalty which Erling converted with ease, then Sa's poor pass out from the back allowed Riyad to intercept and set up Haaland for another goal – and another hat-trick. And of course Erling gets all the headlines – he gets them if he scores a hat-trick, he gets them if he doesn't touch the ball – but how well is Riyad playing? He's benefitted from the rest over the World Cup, but this is the way he's so often been – like the departed Gabriel Jesus, he's a real streaky player, and when he's hot he's really hot. And perhaps more than anyone in the squad, he needs to play regularly to produce his best. Rotation doesn't suit him, but in this team rotation is unavoidable.

Apart from for Haaland. Pep says, 'When he scores I don't know how many hat-tricks and goals, people say he is the solution in our team and when he does not score a goal he is a problem in our team. We know his quality, we know each other. He is not a player to be dropped. We cannot play a false nine with him, we have to adapt with him and I think we are doing quite well.'

And slowly but surely, Haaland seemed to be dragging himself away from his natural habitat to get more involved in the build-up play and make a broader contribution. His goalscoring record is incredible bur Pep's objective for him is to be a much better player when he leaves City than when he arrived. And it's evident from everything that Haaland says that the objective is a shared one.

As encouraging as Erling's return to scoring form had been, an equally warming sight was the form of Jack Grealish, whose confidence and performance levels were edging ever upwards. He was unlucky not to score when Neves headed his fierce effort off the line, but the timid, almost fearful of making a mistake approach was becoming a thing of the past. Now he was taking the ball and immediately getting on the front foot, drawing opponents in and using the space created elsewhere to good effect. It was almost like a switch had been flicked.

But next came a daunting fixture, away at Spurs. Back in the early 2010s, when City were starting to get seriously good, they put together a remarkable sequence of results against a very unremarkable team. At Sunderland's Stadium of Light, they suffered four successive 1-0 defeats. They dominated each and every game but just couldn't find the net, before succumbing to a single goal, usually very late in proceedings. And now, albeit against a rather better side, a similar sequence had emerged. City's record at the Tottenham Hotspur Stadium so far was played four, lost four, scored none. In this time they'd failed to convert two penalties, hit the woodwork twice, suffered from controversially disallowed goals and missed several real sitters. We'd achieved some great results in the final few years of White Hart Lane but this new venue was Kryptonite.

All we could cling to was the fact that these sequences eventually come to an end. In the case of the Stadium of Light, it was Sergio Agüero who finally made the breakthrough, and from then on we won on every subsequent visit. Maybe just one goal here and the same thing will happen. And in terms of incentive, City received a major boost with Arsenal losing at Goodison Park to an Everton side now under Sean Dyche who had replaced the hapless Lampard. You know what to expect when facing a Sean Dyche team but Arsenal still weren't able to cope with it, falling to a 1-0 defeat which opened the door for City to close the gap.

While Haaland was storming inexorably towards the Golden Boot, Harry Kane had just quietly continued to do what he always does. Seldom spectacular but fearsomely efficient, Kane's goal haul had now put him level with Jimmy Greaves, the most naturally gifted goalscorer of his day and arguably any day, as Spurs' all-time leading scorer. Absolutely bloody great. So here he is, needing one goal to break a record which has stood for over 50 years, live in front of the Sky cameras, against the league champions, on a ground where we always struggle. It's not exactly a contender for 'What Happened Next?' is it?

City, not for the first time here, started confidently but failed to find a breakthrough and, again not for the first time, Spurs punished us by scoring with their first attack of note. It wasn't even really much of an attack, more a case of aggressive high pressing forcing an error from Rodri, with Højbjerg transferring the ball for Kane to side-foot past Ederson. A momentous goal for the striker and a predictable, inevitable, sickening one for City to concede.

The nearest we came to breaking the hoodoo was when Mahrez struck the underside of the bar with a crisply struck drive just before half-time, and the second half saw Spurs doggedly hold on, even surviving the dismissal of Romero a few minutes from time. It had been a chastening afternoon for City, a great chance to close the gap squandered and, despite his hat-trick the previous week, the post-match talk, at least on Sky Sports, was all about Haaland and his impact on City's performances.

Jamie Carragher: 'We're waiting for City to kick-in to the City we know so well. It's not the Manchester City of old. It's far easier to counterattack them as well. They are a different team and a lesser team with Erling Haaland, but it's not his fault. Manchester City as a team will not play end-to-end football, it's not Pep Guardiola's way.' And yes, our build-up play is deliberate, precise and structured, but who exactly is going to conjure up end-to-end football against sides which sit deep, defend in numbers and compress the space?'

Carragher continues his rant. 'You think of the goal he got versus West Ham when there was space in behind. I know that's not there every time due to the way City play.' Well not exactly, it's more often not there due to the way our opponents play. 'You saw his blistering pace there – we don't see it here. He might have picked the wrong club to actually get the best out of him.'

Carragher's partner in gratuitous gobshitery Gary Neville also weighs in. 'I remember when Tottenham went 2-0 up at the Etihad a few weeks ago and I said that Pep Guardiola was messing around and tinkering a bit. I felt the same today when I saw the team-sheet come through with no Kevin De Bruyne and Rúben Dias and Aymeric Laporte still on the bench.' City's central defensive pairing today, Aké and Akanji, was the same as played in the 6-3, should have been 10-1, home derby, and you weren't questioning it too much then, Gary.

Neville reckons, 'You can never write Manchester City off. It's almost embarrassing that sometimes you are sat up here saying Guardiola has got it wrong, particularly when proves himself so right so many times like he did a few weeks ago. But something isn't right at Man City. It just feels a little bit strange at the moment.'

It was certainly a rarity to see De Bruyne on the bench for such an important game, but he's never been immune to a temporary loss of form. Who knows how the World Cup, where he was almost unrecognisable, had affected him? Who knows how he's been performing in training? Whether he's got a niggle? The season is long and congested. Pep isn't going to leave him on the bench without good cause. But, for whatever reason, there's no doubt that we're not at our best. Maybe we need something to give us a jolt. Step forward, the Premier League.

Unhappy Interlude

THE MORNING after the Spurs defeat, as we wonder whether and if so when we'll get back to our best, we wake up to a startling headline stating that 'Manchester City are facing the threat of relegation after being charged by the Premier League with more than 100 alleged breaches of financial regulations following a four-year investigation'.

Further reading shows that most of the alleged misdemeanours are the same offence repeated year after year, but nevertheless they're clearly going after us on multiple fronts. Of course, we've been here before, with UEFA hitting us with a two-year European ban before being forced to back down by the Court of Arbitration for Sport. This time, though, we can't have recourse to CAS, and many of the papers report, some with barely disguised glee, that it'll be much harder for us to wriggle out of this one.

The club are quick out of the blocks with a strongly worded riposte, within hours issuing a statement, 'Manchester City FC is surprised by the issuing of these alleged breaches of the Premier League rules, particularly given the extensive engagement and vast amount of detailed materials that the EPL has been provided with. The club welcomes the review of this matter by an independent commission, to impartially consider the comprehensive body of irrefutable evidence that exists in support of its position.

As such we look forward to this matter being put to rest once and for all.'

It's heartening to read, but then we would say that, wouldn't we?

When UEFA originally announced their ban, Pep's response was to potentially distance himself, saying that he would leave if he felt the hierarchy had lied to him. 'When they are accused of something I ask them, "Tell me about that." They explain and I believe them. I said to them, "If you lie to me, the day after I am not here. I will be out and I will not be your friend any more. I put my faith in you because I believe you 100 per cent from day one and I defend the club because of that."' So his press conference before the next game is eagerly awaited. You don't imagine that there'll be too much talk about the actual football. And there isn't.

Pep says, 'My first thought is that we have already been condemned. If we are found to be guilty then we will accept it. But what if we are not guilty? What will be done to remove the damage to our reputation?' In essence, why put these charges in the public domain before we have the chance to defend ourselves? 'We lived it before. It's been like that since Abu Dhabi took the club over. We are not part of the establishment,' he adds.

Pep next trotted out, slowly, deliberately and without prompts, the nine teams to have written to the Court of Arbitration for Sport in March 2020, urging it to suspend City from the Champions League while we appealed our two-year ban. 'Burnley, Wolves, Leicester, Newcastle, Spurs, Arsenal, United, Liverpool, Chelsea.' It was a splendidly theatrical and well-rehearsed performance, Pep next making it clear that he thought the Premier League has now acted under pressure from all 19 of the other clubs. It was us against them.

'Do you think that this has been driven by the other Premier League clubs?'

'Of course.'

'Why do you think that is?'

'I don't know. You will have to ask them, the Daniel Levys and so on.'

'But what will happen if you're found guilty?'

'Then of course we will accept our punishment. But with the UEFA charges we were proved completely innocent, so why should this be different? I'm not moving from this seat. I can assure you. I want to stay here, now more than ever.'

It was robust stuff, even if Pep wasn't quite accurate in his reference to the outcome of the UEFA charges. We weren't exactly exonerated by CAS, rather that some charges were not proven and others were time-barred. Naturally, the fact that some were time-barred led certain people to conclude that if they hadn't been then we'd have been found guilty. And of course not proven doesn't necessarily mean that we were innocent, rather that the prosecutors hadn't quite been able to muster sufficient evidence to send us down. So for our many detractors, the feeling would always remain that we'd got away with it.

Ultimately, UEFA fined us €10m for 'non-cooperation'. Non-cooperation with a body who'd introduced a set of rules specifically targeted at us, designed to prevent us from properly threatening the established elite. An elite whose every penny evidently emanated from organic growth and in no way whatsoever from rich benefactors, exploitation of fans and from a European body who structured its competitions and their rewards in such a way as to ensure that the rich kept on getting richer. Well good for us. And if that's all you've got, can we please move on.

The pretence that Financial Fair Play has anything to do with preventing clubs from going under is almost laughable. Time and again UEFA's motivation has been shown to be to protect the interests of the favoured few, and when those clubs weren't convinced that UEFA's train had quite enough gravy to satisfy their Mr Creosote appetites, they took matters into their own hands, hence the proposal for the European Super League.

Our owners have scarcely put a foot wrong, but allowing themselves to be coerced into joining that group was a serious error of judgment. Yes, we were apparently the last to join and the first to withdraw, and the assumption must be that the choice put before us was join our gang or be left behind as also-rans. This is a far lesser crime than being an instigator, secretly plotting for months if not years how to set this thing up and who to invite, and showing a blatant disregard for the rest of Europe's footballing community, but it was still a mistake and one which was immediately acknowledged.

So why had the Premier League released this bombshell, totally without warning, at this particular time? Could it be a coincidence that a government white paper setting out the road to establishing an independent regulator was imminent? The Premier League needed to show that it could flex its muscles after all, and we were the club chosen to be on the receiving end. But does that mean that everyone else is squeaky clean? Will others face the same level of scrutiny? Pep made veiled reference to that in his press conference, and his former captain Vincent Kompany also offered a succinct but knowing comment. 'I think the football industry in general is not the one to point the finger too many times.'

But for now, we're the only ones in the frame, and it's clear that much of the public, much of the media, has already presumed us guilty. And the longer the process takes, the more they'll assume that we're employing delaying tactics, that we're giving our hotshot lawyers all the time they need to develop the arguments they need to win the day. And maybe we are. Maybe we're hoping that if this thing drags on and on then people will lose the will to keep on fighting against us and just fade away. Pep says, and will reiterate frequently in the coming months, that he wants to see the position resolved as soon as possible. But the likelihood is that it'll take several years and, in the meantime, the very existence of the charges will prompt most commentators to add a caveat when describing our achievements on the pitch.

So what will the impact be on what, for most fans, is and always will be the only thing that really matters? Will the players become distracted, wondering whether they'll be playing in the Vanarama League next season? Based on Pep's performance, it looks that a siege mentality is about to kick in, that we'll be embracing the 'no one likes us, we don't care' ethic that served Ferguson so well at Old Trafford. Rather than distracting the players it might instead serve to galvanise them, to make them even more focused and determined.

Do we care if no one likes us? Personally I've always cared very much. Prior to the takeover, in those days when we were no threat to anyone other than the mental health of our own supporters, it was difficult for people other than United fans to dislike City; indeed we went out of our way to make ourselves the source of endless hilarity among the football community. No one cocked it up quite as well or quite as often as we did. But how things change when you come into money.

The resentment came from two sources. Firstly the fact that we'd suddenly got more money than everyone else and secondly where it emanated from. I've never resented lottery winners. It's how you react to it that matters. Turn into Billy Big Bollocks, go around giving it large, treating old friends like they're suddenly beneath you, then you deserve all the contempt you get. But I genuinely don't think we've done that. The word Pep uses more than any other in describing positive characteristics of his players is 'humble' and I struggle to recall when anyone connected with the club gave an interview which didn't convey this quality. They're media-trained all right, but there's no doubt that this is a genuine core value for Pep. I remember him publicly admonishing Raheem Sterling after he tried a few showboating step-overs towards the end of a game already well won. He could have waited until they were back in the dressing room, but he chose to do it on the pitch, straight after the final whistle, to let everyone know what was expected. Respect the opposition and don't go round taking the piss.

The 'where the money came from' is another thing entirely. Let's just say that when it comes to folk from the Middle East, stereotypical prejudices are not unheard of.

But at least there are some people on our side, and not just City supporters. FFP was designed to pull up a drawbridge, to make it impossible for anyone other than the established big boys to compete consistently. You might get the occasional blip – Leicester City being the most notable example – but a blip is all it will ever be. In fact, the governing bodies would welcome a Leicester every now and then, so they can use it as evidence to support an argument that the regime is working just fine, that any team outside the elite can still win the big prizes. But sustaining that success? Forget it. Leicester essentially remained a selling club, and slowly but surely fell away.

Writing in *The Times*, Martin Samuel put a nice counterpoint to the concept of asterisks being put against the names of trophy-winning sides if they're subsequently shown to have broken the rules. 'This league was won,' the asterisk would indicate, 'under protectionist regulations known as Financial Fair Play. These prevented owners investing fully in their businesses, making the established elite clubs stronger and weakening their smaller opponents. The clubs that stood to gain the most helped to shape these rules in which limits were placed on ambition and the potential for competition. Do most modern Premier League owners have the funds to finance investment in their project? Yes. Are they allowed? No. Because they cannot grow in any significant way they must sit, ripe for plunder, as their best players are taken away piecemeal.'

Samuel went on to point out that it was actually Chelsea who were the original targets of FFP, but by the time the rules were in place, they had their feet under the table and were so cosy that Roman Abramovich actually supported the regulations as a way of keeping City at bay. The classic poacher turned gamekeeper.

An unlikely supporter of Samuel's view was Gary Neville. 'I've got a real problem with FFP, I've had it for a long time. It was driven through by the established elite so that clubs like City, clubs like Chelsea, couldn't compete with them – basically they can always pat them on the head and say "stay down there".'

Of course, just because you don't like the rules doesn't give you the right to trample all over them, but when they're so blatantly constructed with such a protectionist objective, there are certainly mitigating circumstances. Has there been the same antagonism towards Newcastle and their new Saudi owners? It doesn't feel like it to me, but maybe that's because they haven't won anything yet. But I welcome it. Not just because it gives the witless internet trolls another target to throw their 'sportswashing' jibes at, but because the more competitive the league the better. The more teams able to bring in top players, the better. The more matches there'll be with a real sense of jeopardy, and the fewer afternoons spent watching us try to break down sides who feel their only chance of getting a result is to stack the defence, waste time from minute one and bore the pants off 50,000 spectators who've spent a fair few bob for their afternoon's viewing. And if that means we don't win so much, or don't win anything at all, then we'll have to find a way to improve, just as it should be.

Nevertheless, for the foreseeable future, we'll be playing under a cloud. But coming from Manchester we're well used to that.

15 February 2023, Premier League: Arsenal 1 City 3

'We have to play a little bit more like this sometimes'

OUR FIRST game after the Premier League's bombshell was at home to Aston Villa. With City fans fired up by the charges, the club's unequivocal denials and Pep's powerful response in the press conference, the tone for the afternoon had been set. The fans were in full-on 'us versus them' mode, with the Premier League anthem being roundly booed and banners and chants of defiance in plentiful evidence. Compared with recent fixtures, the atmosphere was pumped, with the fans at their most supportive and raucous, and it spilled over to the players as City made a rousing start to the game. In just the fourth minute, Rodri sprinted to the near post to meet Mahrez's corner, and his powerful glancing header squeezed past Martínez.

For the first time in a while, we were properly on it from the start but, despite some enterprising approach play, we couldn't build on the lead until five minutes before half-time, when Haaland's ridiculous pace saw him surge on to De Bruyne's deflected through ball. Although he couldn't reach it in time to get a shot away, he skilfully made the room to fire in a crisp low cross for Gündoğan to tap in at the far post. An outstanding assist for Haaland; a very familiar, perfectly timed run into space from Gundo.

When Grealish then provoked a clumsy challenge from Ramsey, it was Mahrez who, surprisingly given their respective recent records, stepped up instead of Haaland to take the penalty. This time he sent Martínez the wrong way to give City a commanding lead and allow Pep to make a couple of half-time changes, clearly with the trip to the Emirates in three days' time very much on his mind.

And it seemed to be on the players' minds as well, as they slipped into game management mode. A mistake from Bernardo allowed Watkins to burst through and slide the ball past Ederson's arthritic attempt to get down, and there were a couple of close shaves for City to endure before finally sealing the points. But it was job done and got everyone – well, most people – talking about matters on the pitch again, as the big night at the Emirates loomed into focus.

It's Arsenal's biggest match for years. They're three points ahead of us with a game in hand. If they win tonight, it'll be worth much more than just the three points. We've beaten them in every one of our last 11 meetings in the league; the belief they'd get from finally putting one over us would be unquantifiable. For them it's the ultimate test. Arteta had shied away from putting their strongest side up against us in the FA Cup, but now there was no hiding place for his young stars, the would-be heirs to our throne. It was time for them to show us what they'd got.

In that cup tie, they'd operated a very effective high press, supported by aggressive man-for-man marking. Pep had been surprised then, but if they do it again tonight, how will we deal with it? With the crowd creating a frenzied atmosphere, Arsenal start on the front foot with Saka particularly lively. What a fabulous talent this boy is. Is it a wise move for Pep to put Bernardo at left-back? Presumably he's seeking more creative ways for us to play out but, for all his qualities, Bernardo looks seriously exposed. This is not quite the solution to Cancelo's departure that most of us envisaged.

It's a game of pace, and Arsenal's attempts to make it difficult to build from the back are dealt with in a different way from the recent cup tie. Rather than the super-patient back and forth trying to play through the press – an approach fraught with danger, especially away from home with the crowd urging them to push on to us even more aggressively – we're happy to mix it up and from time to time play the long ball towards Haaland. Initially he doesn't win too many of them, but he brings Saliba and Gabriel away from their comfort zone, also creating space to play should we win the second ball.

After Arsenal miss a great chance to take the lead, the unmarked Nketiah heading wide from just seven yards, we get what we need to dampen the atmosphere, and it's the long ball to Haaland which starts the process. He pressurises Saliba into glancing the ball backwards, forcing Tomiyasu to back pedal with Grealish snapping energetically at his heels, doing everything he can to force a mistake. And he succeeds, as the defender's back-pass to Ramsdale is under-hit. De Bruyne has surged forward in anticipation of just such an eventuality and gets there before the keeper, instantly sizing up the options before clipping the ball over his head and watching it curl beautifully into the net. Even though replays show that he struck the ball with his ankle, the manner of the finish is precisely what he intended. If Rooney can be feted forever for his overhead shinner in 2011, for sure Kev should get full credit for this one.

Arsenal get level in contentious circumstances, as Nketiah comes in from the left and clips the ball past Ederson from a tight angle. Aké manages to clear the ball off the line, but the relief is short-lived as Anthony Taylor points to the spot. Taylor deems that Ederson had clattered into Nketiah after he'd got the shot away. There's certainly a coming together, unseen by most spectators as they followed the path of the ball, but while City protest that Ederson made no attempt to impede the striker, that he could hardly vanish into thin air, had a similar incident occurred outside the box it would be a free kick every time. In the modern game it's a nailed-on spot-kick. Saka is charged with the responsibility, and coolly sends Eddie the wrong way to bring the scores level. Arsenal's display deserves it, but City still almost go in ahead as Rodri's header deflects off Aké and rebounds off the bar.

The penalty incident has definitely upped the level of intensity on the pitch and in the stands, and for the first part of the second half the game is particularly fractious, resembling the many title-defining Arsenal-United encounters of the Ferguson-Wenger era. Every decision by Taylor sees him surrounded by a horde of angry, dissenting players, and the game gets ugly and scrappy. The revelation in this phase is Haaland, as he progressively gets more on top of the Arsenal centre-backs, bullying them, bringing team-mates into play. It's a real old-style centre-forward display, Haaland clearly relishing the physical battle and showing a facet of his game that has seldom been seen – or needed – before tonight. These are two sides renowned for their fluid passing games, but this is a scrap.

When Haaland powers away from Gabriel, he's dragged to the ground inside the area and Taylor duly points to the spot. But after the obligatory VAR check, Erling is found to have been marginally offside, giving the Gunners a reprieve. Pep then replaces Mahrez with Akanji, on the face of it a defensive move but it's one which frees Bernardo to take up a more conventional position, while also giving us a more solid look at the back.

Incidents like the overturned penalty can be as good as a goal in terms of their effect on the crowd, but City carry on regardless and increasingly look the more likely to score the next goal. And it comes when Haaland seizes on the ball, playing into Gündoğan on the edge of the area and sprinting forward for a possible return. But Gundo knows what's around him and instead allows the ball to pass through to Grealish, coming in from the left. It's a decent chance, and Jack strikes the ball with that familiar side-foot towards the far corner. The direction is telegraphed and Ramsdale anticipates, but the ball takes a slight deflection off Tomiyasu, bounces into the ground and passes over the keeper into the net. It's our most important goal of the season so far and Grealish celebrates accordingly in front of the City fans. It means a lot to us, and a lot to him. He had a bit of luck, but his performance deserves it.

We're properly on top now, and soon make it count. Walker forces Trossard into coughing up possession and a quick interchange sees Gundo play De Bruyne through on the right. Kev quickly fizzes a low cut-back to Haaland, who's found some space 12 yards out. Haaland controls the ball with his left foot and in an instant strikes a low drive with his right into Ramsdale's far corner. It's not his usual one-touch finish but it feels like it, the speed with which he gets his shot away preventing Saliba from closing him down and not allowing Ramsdale to set himself for a possible save. It's a phenomenal demonstration of the striker's art, the coordination needed to execute it truly extraordinary.

Nketiah misses a late chance to set up a thrilling finale but by then Arsenal fans are streaming out of the ground, shamefully having given up the ghost on a side whose performances this season have been consistently outstanding. It's a great result, demonstrating our capacity to find another way of winning, and City are top of the league, even though Arsenal have a game in hand. And if the defeat affects the belief of Mikel Arteta's team as much as it seems to have damaged that of their fans, then a third title in a row is definitely on the cards.

But Arteta begs to differ. 'I have more belief than I had before the game. With the performance and the level the team put in, we had the feeling we could beat them. Until the second goal we had them. But we gave them three goals. The difference was in the boxes, they had three chances and they put them away. We had chances and we didn't put them away.'

I hate it when managers say this. They gave us three goals? No they didn't. They made mistakes which ultimately led to three goals. If you track back far enough, every goal ever scored emanates from an opposition mistake. It's not the same thing as giving them a goal. Tomiyasu's mistake was the closest to it, but then Kev was hardly left with a tap-in; how else would it have made the shortlist for *Match of the Day*'s Goal of the Month? And the other two goals featured superb passing movements and in Haaland's case an astonishing finish. Pep himself was clear on what had made the difference. 'Haaland helped us a lot by being man-to-man and being aggressive. Playing long balls against Saliba and Gabriel is not easy but he used his body to win the balls. And that's why we won the game.'

If the tactic of playing long to Haaland had been a great success, the experiment with Bernardo wasn't quite such a winner for Pep. 'In the first half, I tried something new and it was horrible! ... we adjusted in the second half and we were more aggressive towards Ødegaard and controlled more of the ball ... Erling used his power to keep the ball ... Bernardo Silva started at left-back and finished as right-winger ... few players can do that!'

And it was a very un-City like performance, with just 36 per cent possession. 'We have to play a little bit more like this sometimes and that is what we did today,' said Haaland and, while he may not have won the highest percentage of long balls played in his direction, picking up second balls was something we were prepared for – and proved to be very good at. And then we made the most of it. To set up the way Arsenal did takes a lot of bravery and not many other teams are likely to do it. But if they do, we know we've got a weapon to combat it. I don't think we'll be turning into the new Wimbledon just yet, but it doesn't hurt to let future opponents know that Pep has a Plan B after all.

16

4 March 2023, Premier League: City 2 Newcastle 0

'Phil is our diamond'

THE ARSENAL result established City as clear title favourites and was widely expected to trigger one of those familiar relentless winning runs, especially with the next few fixtures looking particularly inviting. The first of them took City to the City Ground to face a Forest side fighting hard to avoid an immediate return to the Championship. They'd been battered 6-0 at the Etihad back in August, but their survival chances were always going to depend on their home form and they came into this game unbeaten in their previous seven at the City Ground.

City looked set to get a pre-match boost with the result from Villa Park, where suggestions that Arsenal's challenge might crumble after their midweek defeat were given credence as they trailed Villa 2-1 at half-time. Even when they equalised they still looked set to drop points, but deep into injury time they had an outrageous stroke of luck, Jorginho's shot coming back off the bar, hitting keeper Emi Martínez on the way out and rebounding into the net. What would have been their fourth winless game instead ended up giving them a huge lift, the messages coming from Arteta and his men afterwards full of defiance. And their afternoon would soon get even better.

City were dominant from the start at the City Ground, but it was almost half-time before Bernardo's 20 yarder seared past Navas to give us the lead our total control – 84 per cent possession against a side sitting deep with ten men consistently behind the ball – had deserved. Now it was a question of getting the second and putting the game to bed and, with Forest at least occasionally trying to commit men forward, the chances to do so came. And went.

When Foden was put through on Navas with Haaland racing up alongside him a goal looked certain, but Phil got caught in two minds, stumbled at the crucial moment and mishit his attempted pass. Raheem Sterling couldn't have done it better himself. Then from five yards out, absolutely central, Laporte had a free header as he steamed in to meet De Bruyne's corner but planted it straight at Navas. Finally, when Foden's drive was spilled by Navas, Haaland latched on to the rebound only to fire against the bar. That was bad enough, but the ball came back to him and, after chesting it down, he contrived to blaze it over the top, to roars of delight from the home support.

Navas made a great save to tip Gündoğan's free kick over the top but as the clock ran down it still looked as though one goal would be enough, with Forest not having mustered a shot on target. But then, a smart move down the right and a couple of missed tackles saw Gibbs-White get free and his low cross was tapped home at the far post by Chris Wood. It was a proper smash-and-grab, with City having created more clear chances than for many a week but paying a heavy price for having one of those days up front. And it felt as though much of the good work at the Emirates had been undone, with Arsenal back in control of their own destiny as well as getting the boost to morale that added time winning goals always bring.

Sky's Laura Hunter summed it up. 'A week that began with so much promise – outshining Arsenal on their own patch – has ended in regret. This was the moment to seize control of the title race and City stuttered. How they might come to rue those opportunities missed.'

It felt like a brief flashback to Typical City, but Pep was philosophical. 'It was a really good game,' he told *Match of the Day*. 'We did everything, we played perfectly, had amazing chances, we were going to see the game out, we couldn't believe it, but this is football. You have to score. It's one of the best games we've played but we dropped two points. It happens, it's football.'

Match of the Day have taken to showing the expected goals (xG) figures for each fixture, and the numbers for this game came out at 3.21 to 0.86 in our favour which, at least as I understood it, suggests that based on the chances created we should have won the game 3-1. But for some reason this piques my interest and I trawl the net to find out exactly how xG is calculated. What I discover is that it's the expected number of goals from the shots actually taken rather than from the chances created. This is not the same thing at all.

When Phil was put through with Erling alongside him, with just Navas to beat, you'd imagine it would end up in a goal say 60 or 70 per cent of the time, so we'd be credited with an xG of say 0.6 to 0.7. But Phil stumbled and didn't get a pass away and, because we ended up not attempting a shot at all, our credited xG for this incident, this glorious clear-cut opportunity, was zero. If Phil instead had taken a shot, the xG might have been say 0.5, the likelihood of beating a keeper in a one-on-one. If he'd drawn the keeper out and rolled the ball across to Erling, leaving the striker with a completely vacant net to tap the ball into from a yard out, the xG would have been maybe 0.99, reflecting the likelihood that Erling would score with a shot from that position. (You never know, he might have done a Ronnie Rosenthal.) So depending on the choice made by Foden, the xG credited for this opportunity could have been anything between 0 and 0.99. But it's the same chance, two of them bearing down on an unprotected keeper.

As an indicator of which team 'ought to have won' – which is how it's usually interpreted – xG is to be taken with a bucketful of salt. It might be useful for estimating how many goals an individual player should have scored from the shots they attempted, but even then it's obviously flawed – what if they don't attempt a shot when they could have done? What if they try to go round the keeper rather than slide the ball past him? This obsession with stats is not healthy. Trying to assign static data to such a fluid game just doesn't work. It might be fun, and give people something to talk about, but it's not even remotely reliable. Back in the distant days when I was doing sums at school, they called this kind of thing 'spurious accuracy'. That's maths-speak for Absolute Bollocks. And when it comes to football, you can throw all the scientific analysis you like at it, there's only one statistic that really matters. The same one that's only ever mattered.

A week later City travelled for a third successive away league game – and a fifth in all competitions – and the pressure was on to avoid another slip-up. Bournemouth felt like ideal opposition, still looking for their first point in a Premier League game against City. And they wouldn't be breaking their duck this afternoon. The clinical edge was back, with Foden at the heart of everything. He was involved in all four goals, and even though none of them could be described as beautiful it was the perfect way to put the previous week's frustrations behind us.

Álvarez prodded home after Haaland had struck the bar, before Erling himself tapped home after Foden knocked the ball across the face of goal. Phil then got on the scoresheet for the first time since the World Cup with an emphatic finish after being gifted the ball by Philip Billing, and early in the second half an Álvarez drive was deflected in off Mepham. With City understandably moving into game management mode after a gruelling schedule, Lerma pulled a late goal back to the intense irritation of the City defenders – and Ederson, who otherwise would have registered his 100th clean sheet for the club. The excellent Rico Lewis, allowed already to be interviewed after games, said he was 'gutted' not to keep a clean sheet, with Pep again talking up his performance afterwards. And Foden came in for particular praise. 'No one can doubt Phil! He is still young but his work ethic is always there. Sometimes he is not brilliant like he usually is but I am sure this goal will help him.'

The point was made to Pep that even at 4-0 up, the likes of Haaland, Foden and Grealish were working back, making interceptions in our own penalty area even when the game was essentially won. 'They would be in trouble if they didn't do it,' he smiled. 'When the fans spend five or six hours in their car to come here and pay for a ticket, and our players with their salaries, we have to run when even it's 3-0 or 4-0.'

So would *this* be the result to launch the winning run we needed? So far our longest sequence of victories in the league was just three games. As we moved into March, that needed to change, with Arsenal seemingly over their little blip, and once again five points clear.

* * *

Newcastle arrived at the Etihad having just lost the Carabao Cup Final to United, despite having generally had the better of the play. It's 54 years since they last won a trophy. We know how they feel; well, almost. We managed just the 35. But at least they don't have to put up with gloating neighbours piling up the trophies and mocking them at every turn. Will they be flat or will their Wembley defeat just make them redouble their efforts to get a Champions League spot?

It doesn't start too well for them as City almost score in the first minute, some increasingly familiar build-up play ending with Grealish's dinked cross being headed just over by the late-arriving Gündoğan. But within a few minutes we're ahead as Foden hits his fourth goal in eight days, a thrilling slalom seeing him carve his way past two Newcastle defenders before slotting past Nick Pope, albeit with the aid of a deflection. This was Foden at his absolute best, the sort of thing only he can do, an almost daredevil incursion through the heart of the defence.

Newcastle start to pose their own threat, and Longstaff looks certain to equalise only to be denied by a superb sliding block from Aké, who's emerging as our most impressive and reliable defender. And there are other chances, Wilson miskicking from eight yards out, right in front of goal, and Joelinton faring even worse from a similar position, failing to make any contact at all with the goal at his mercy.

If not exactly on the ropes, City were living dangerously, and Guardiola brought on Bernardo in a bid to orchestrate longer periods of possession. What we got instead was a second goal, as within just two minutes Bernardo ran on to Haaland's clever flick to plant the ball low past Pope from the edge of the box. Once again a Pep substitution had produced a vital goal almost instantly, and this one broke Newcastle's resistance. It wasn't City's best or most fluent performance – according to *The Guardian*'s hard-to-please Jamie Jackson 'flat, discordant and ending in a scrappy win that would have been a blazing, rampant victory in previous seasons' – but given the quality of the opposition and the fact that we were coming off the back of five consecutive away games, it was still a terrific result.

The competition for places was intense all over the pitch. Mahrez had been consistently excellent since the World Cup, Foden had stormed back to top form, Grealish was now really affecting games, his confidence fully restored and with far more end product. A popular topic of conversation among City fans was, 'If we had a Champions League final next week, what would Pep's starting 11 be?' Other than Ederson, Rodri, De Bruyne and Haaland, the other places would be up for grabs. Which is surely exactly as Pep would want it.

* * *

It had been a real treat to see Foden back to this kind of form. For whatever reason, he'd struggled after returning from the World Cup, almost the first blip in a senior career of continuous improvement. But Pep had never doubted that he'd be back. 'If you are saying I don't trust Phil, forget about it. Phil is our diamond. He needs to be himself. I saw other players better than him at times after the World Cup. I'm pretty sure Phil will go up and down. At his age, what do you expect? It's going to happen. When it does it's how you come back to the principles and in that moment he will be a better player.

'Phil has this special ability to go up there, attack with the ball, attack without the ball. But earlier in the year, when he had the ball he was passing back, passing back. I said, "Phil you don't have the confidence to do it. You have to have the confidence to be direct."' And much of it was down to being less than 100 per cent fit, playing through a foot injury. Pep said, 'He made an incredible effort, playing with pain, and arrived at a moment when he said, "Pep, I cannot play any more," so he had to rest. We gave him a week or two off, and after that Riyad Mahrez was in his best time of the season and Jack Grealish made a step forward.

'I said, "What happened to you Phil is absolutely normal. Because you arrived at 17 years old training with us, ten, 15, 20 minutes here and there. Then national team, World Cup, European Cup, winning titles; every year a little bit better, a little bit better. Then for a moment you go down a level, so you have to accept it, don't blame others, the opponent or the manager or the club. Accept that you can do better and step by step you will be back and scoring goals. I say to him, 'You are so young, if you drop a little bit this season, it's an absolutely normal process.'

And that's all there is to it. 'He is training like an animal, no doubt about that, and he will be back, like he was at Nottingham, where he was brilliant.'

* * *

With our game having been chosen for the lunchtime slot, we can enjoy a relaxing Saturday afternoon in the pub, knowing that we've got the three points necessary to stay within striking distance, although with Arsenal having what looks like a straightforward assignment at home to Bournemouth, we wouldn't expect to close the gap. But Bournemouth score after just a few seconds and not only hold on until half-time but increase their lead just before the hour mark.

We don't have too much time to get excited, as within 12 minutes the Gunners are back on level terms and with 20 minutes plus added time to go, we assume that there's only one outcome and order another beer. But you never know. Bournemouth somehow navigate the 20 minutes and all that remains is the added time. There's six minutes of it but Arsenal get a corner well into the seventh of them and they're allowed to take it. The ball comes out to the edge of the area, Reiss Nelson lashes it home and everyone goes ballistic. Added time on added time is the norm these days and it's usually totally justified. Doesn't make it any easier to swallow though.

There are serious scenes at the Emirates. They're getting a bit giddy. You'd think it was an Agüero moment. The excitement's understandable but isn't it a bit early to be reacting quite so wildly? Yes, they only have their league games left to worry about while we're still going strong in three competitions, but the emotional energy these guys are expending can't be helping them. For the second week running they've come from behind to win in added time. There's nothing that feels better at the time, but it takes so much out of you. They can't keep doing it. Can they?

* * *

The final Premier League game before the international break takes us to Selhurst Park. Patrick Vieira's team are in a real slump, their previous nine games having delivered no wins and just four goals. They failed to register a shot on target in either of the last two. They've sunk perilously close to the relegation zone and Vieira is under serious pressure.

City start with real purpose, Rodri's ferocious early volley forcing Guaita into a superb save, before an incisive run by Grealish ends with him dragging his shot just wide.

The first half's best chance falls to Haaland, but as he tries to clip Aké's cross into the vacant goal he gets under the ball and it clears the crossbar. Palace, meanwhile, produce nothing. Nothing at all. By far the most unambitious side we've faced all season – and there've been a few – their strategy is evidently to sit deep, work hard and hope we keep on missing.

And we do. With Foden strangely out of sorts after such a good run and De Bruyne resting on the bench ahead of our Champions League tie, we struggle for creativity as the clock ticks down. We need a moment of inspiration or a helping hand. It's the latter which comes to our rescue. When Gündoğan receives a short corner, Palace aren't quite ready and, in his rush to close İlkay down, Michael Olise clatters into him after he's played the ball back to Grealish. It's an obvious penalty and despite having been nowhere near his best, Haaland calmly strokes it home for the vital goal.

Palace huff and puff in a belated bid to put us under pressure, but the game ends with them yet again having had no shots on target and shortly afterwards Vieira is dismissed. And on the basis of this wretched performance from his team, you wouldn't call it unexpected. It's been the definition of one of those fixtures where you have to grind it out, find a way to get the three points and put the game out of your head. For most City fans, that would be accomplished the moment they passed through the exit gates.

17

5 March 2023, Premier League: Liverpool 7 Manchester United 0

'It was a great day for British football'

OK, SO this bit isn't actually about a City game, but how could you possibly leave it out?

One of my favourite rhymes in the whole of pop music comes in the Ramones' 'Teenage Lobotomy' – 'Now I guess I've gotta tell 'em that I've got no cerebellum.' Unfortunately, whenever I hear it, I automatically think of Robbie Savage. This is word association at its most profoundly depressing. After United have claimed the Carabao Cup – a Mickey Mouse competition for their supporters except when they win it – Savage tells those BBC Radio 5 listeners without the wherewithal to locate their 'Off' button that Ten Hag is the best manager in the world and that United could win four trophies this season. This is a bit like saying the Monster Raving Loony Party could win every single seat at the next general election. It's theoretically possible but it's not going to happen. His employers justify Savage's retention by the fact that he apparently gets people talking. But what they're usually saying is how does this self-obsessed half-witted numpty get to pollute our airwaves so frequently?

The day after our win over Newcastle, Liverpool host United and as usual it's built up by Sky as *the* big game of the season. United are still within striking distance – if they win their games in hand they'll be just three points behind us – and there are plenty, not just Savage, giving it large about how wonderful they are, how they'll keep their run going and turn out to be Arsenal's main challengers. To my possibly slightly biased eyes, they've ridden their luck on so many occasions and their elevated position is a false reflection of their quality. But this is no consolation; indeed, if anything it makes matters worse. Their history is littered with undeserved successes. And the fear is that they're about to embark on another era of unmerited glory.

If they win at Anfield they'll be bloody unbearable, and in doing so will also have negotiated their most difficult remaining fixture. And certainly the one they'd most love to win. But they don't win. They lose 7-0. SEVEN–NIL. It's not just my favourite game of the season so far, it's one of my favourite games of all time. To watch them disintegrate in such spectacular fashion is a thing of wonder, and as their afternoon goes from bad to worse you get a true indication of the true personality of some of their players. And one of them in particular.

They've had some contemptible characters over the years but Bruno Fernandes is right up there with the very worst of them. If you typed 'petulant whining prima donna' into an online thesaurus his name would emerge as the closest match. And here his sulky, childish behaviour reaches a new level, looking accusingly at his team-mates as the goals go in while he himself lets players go past without any attempt to tackle or track back. When Ten Hag is preparing to make a substitution, Fernandes looks across pleadingly, desperate to be taken off. It's a pathetic display. And he's the bloody captain! When the going gets tough, the petulant start flouncing, and this man is a world-class flouncer.

'The second half has been an absolute disgrace, a shambles, epitomised by Bruno Fernandes who has been embarrassing,' said Gary Neville on Sky Sports. 'Some of Fernandes's behaviour in the second half has been a disgrace. He is holding his hands up asking, "Why am I not coming off?" I've had enough of him not running back, he whinges at everybody … he got pushed in the chest and goes down holding his face.'

Chris Sutton echoes the sentiments. 'Bruno Fernandes, take a bow for one of the worst performances we have seen from a Premier League player, certainly from a captain … It was more befitting a petulant child.'

There's a marvellous set-to after the game, in a studio tag-team contest featuring Souness and Carragher vs Neville and Keane. Neville's technique when losing an argument is to dig his heels in, insist he's right by repeating himself again and again and try to belittle the other protagonist. It was illustrated perfectly after their 4-0 drubbing at Brentford, when he was adamant that the Glazers should get the next plane over and explain themselves to United's fans. Jamie Redknapp not unreasonably suggested that the performance of the players might have been a bigger factor in the humiliation, but this was dismissed out of hand. After all, Redknapp never played for The World's Greatest Football Club ™, so what did he know?

And now he's at it again. 'It's a freak result,' he pleads, insistent that United are on the right track. Souness counters with, 'It's not a freak result, it could have been more than seven, they've got away lightly here today, I think they've been getting away with it. They got beat six at Man City, four at Brentford, were they freak results as well?' While

Neville foams at the mouth, Keane simply smirks. Even he knows there's no point getting involved in an argument you can't win. Meanwhile, Bruno Fernandes, Captain Fantastic, steps up for an interview, claiming, 'We've had worse moments than this.' Bloody hell, I wish I'd seen them.

After the match, Sky show footage of Carragher and Neville seated together, and their contrasting reactions as each of the goals goes in. It's a low bar but in my view this is Carragher's finest ever TV moment. And Noel Gallagher summed up the feelings of City fans everywhere. 'It was a great day for British football. The only sad thing about it is it was them that beat 'em.'

The following day, I'm still in a fuzzy 7-0 dreamland as I meet up with my good pal Shaun for a few beers and a late lunch. He's in a similarly mellow mood, being as he is a lifelong Liverpool fan. We share a common enemy. We've had a couple of gentle beers and are heading down towards Deansgate's finest steakhouse, chatting about what an utter prat Gobshite Gary made himself look and what a piece of work he is in general. And then, as we look up, walking towards us is the self-same Gary Neville. We do a double take but it's unmistakably him, side by side with a woman who we assume is a business contact.

The very sight of him prompts an involuntary burst of raucous laughter as he walks past us, laughter which continues as we carry on our separate ways. But then, as I glance over my shoulder, he does an about turn and storms back towards us with a display of aggressive walking that would put Kevin Horlock to shame. And he's seriously confrontational. 'What the fuck are you laughing at?' he asks, giving us the hard stare that put the fear of God into so many over the years. Well, maybe not that many. We're both totally gobsmacked, partly at what a tiny, insignificant figure he cuts but also at this extraordinary reaction. He really looks like he wants to take us on. Who does he think he is? He clearly takes himself very seriously indeed, a 'don't you know who I am?' merchant if ever I saw one. And in his eyes, laughing at Manchester United is a very serious offence indeed.

It's one of those moments where in the hours to come I'll think of so many things that I wish I'd said, but at the time none of them sprang to mind. Instead I just say, 'What a coincidence, we were just talking about you,' and it's a benign enough response for him to back down, realise what an absolute dickhead he's been, and carry on with his day.

Our own day continues with a couple of monster ribeyes, washed down with more red wine than doctors conventionally recommend, and we then head to the Northern Quarter for a couple of beers in the legendary Millstone pub. It's Karaoke Central seven days a week and, although Shaun is normally a most reluctant performer, I put his name down for 'You'll Never Walk Alone'. The combination of alcohol and a glowing sense of well-being is just enough for him to take up the challenge.

It's possibly a minor misjudgement. Belting out the Liverpool anthem in a central Manchester pub the day after they've drubbed United 7-0, with those poor sensitive souls still raw after the humiliation at the hands of their most bitter rivals could be regarded as being slightly inflammatory.

He's absolutely bloody terrible. I'm recording his performance on my phone, providing backing vocals from the floor, and they're even worse. But despite the ungodly racket, I can hear a few growls behind me, and the tone is distinctly unfriendly: 'That's not right!' and 'Leave it! Leave it!' I glance back and can see that there's a guy at the bar getting seriously agitated.

As Shaun finishes his epic performance this guy comes up and starts jostling him. He's extremely aggressive, his anger evidently fuelled by a beer or nine, and he demands to know why we're singing the Liverpool anthem. To be honest I'm amazed he recognised it. I say we don't mean anything by it, it's just a really nice song. It's not the most convincing argument, but our evidently placid and non-confrontational nature just about allows us to get away with it as he storms out of the pub. How bitter can you get? But we conclude that the rest of our evening might be better spent downing a few quiet pints in the corner rather than being tempted to treat the Monday night crowd to any further classics from The Great Anfield Songbook. Sometimes, self-preservation has to take priority.

18

14 March 2023, Champions League: City 7 RB Leipzig 0

'A man drowning in honey'

IN THE Champions League, the last-16 draw paired us with RB Leipzig, sitting third in the Bundesliga. The first leg allowed us a visit their charming home town, although a one-day local transport strike – presumably laid on by those considerate German folk just so we could feel at home – means that we face a fair old schlep to get to the Red Bull Arena.

As ever in Germany, it's a cracking atmosphere but City, despite the absence of the unwell Kevin De Bruyne, completely dominate first-half possession, finally going ahead with another slick finish from Riyad Mahrez. It looks like being a straightforward evening but the second period sees Leipzig show much more ambition – and aggression – and we struggle to respond. After a couple of close shaves, they equalise through their highly rated and apparently much-coveted centre-back Joško Gvardiol and if anything look the more likely to nick a winner.

Haaland has an off-night, screwing a decent chance well wide late on, although right at the death there's a strange incident when what looks like a blatant handball by a Leipzig defender is followed by the sound of the referee blowing the full-time whistle. That, of course, shouldn't matter, as the VAR team will presumably review the incident. Instead, it seems as though they've already buggered off for a cup of tea as no review is forthcoming. It's a strange episode, as by the standards being set this season it's an obvious penalty and would probably have been given even in the far more sensible days of yore.

It feels like a disappointing outcome, a conclusion certainly supported by the body language of the players at the end, but Pep is quickly out there, saying, 'Why are your heads down? Get your heads up. It was really good the way you played. If people don't like it, it doesn't matter.' And he was prickly when talking to BT Sport later. 'You expect us to come here and win 5-0? That is not a reality.' The problem is that people do expect us to go to places like this and win 5-0. It felt strange that Pep didn't make any substitutions, the first time this has happened in any Champions League game for almost five years, and it suggested that we were happy enough to take a draw. We didn't used to do that. But then we didn't used to win the Champions League either.

So, it's a decent result, but unlike in recent seasons means that the return leg at the Etihad is far from a formality, with no chance of resting the legs of some of those who could do with a bit of a breather. It's our first home game since the Anfield Massacre and I notice with a smile that the shelves in the concourse bars contain a healthy supply of 7-Up. Maybe they've always been there, it's just that they seem to have a bit more meaning at the moment.

It has the potential to be a difficult night but City get an early helping hand from VAR, with the referee being sent to the monitor to review another possible handball for which not one City player appealed. It was the sort of decision the pundits consistently call disgraceful, ignoring the fact that it's the rules – or at least the way the officials are instructed to interpret them – which are the real problem. There was nothing intentional about the handball – it was from very close range, the ball merely brushed the defender's arm and he wasn't even looking at it. But under the existing regime none of this matters at all.

Haaland emphatically accepted the gift, and within less than a minute he added a second, in so doing providing another indication of how his game was evolving. He hurtled 20 yards to close down keeper Blaswich, forcing him into a rushed clearance which was instantly volleyed back forward by Akanji, stationed in the centre circle. In that time Haaland had sprinted to get himself back onside, and nodded the ball back to De Bruyne, some 30 yards out. Kev took a couple of touches to tame the bouncing ball, before unleashing a savage left-footer which dipped and crashed down off the underside of the bar. Moving in at full pelt to pounce was Haaland, who leapt athletically, spectacularly, thrillingly, in the style of a Michael Jordan slam dunk, to head the ball at the top of the bounce into an empty net.

The game had been transformed, although Ederson had a crazy minute when he firstly sprinted out of his goal to clatter Werner, who inexplicably was booked for diving, and then passed the ball straight to a Leipzig player, who failed to find a team-mate in front of the vacant goal. But City remained by far the more threatening, Blaswich keeping them just afloat with a couple of top-drawer saves until, just before half-time, a Dias header hit the inside of the post, and rolled all the way back across the line. Following in was Haaland, forcing Haidara's attempted clearance into the net to complete his fifth Etihad hat-trick of the season and render the second half a formality.

It was still an immensely enjoyable one. Within a few minutes the scoreline approached rout proportions, a flowing Ederson, Bernardo, De Bruyne, Gündoğan, Grealish move culminating in a return pass to Gundo being drilled low into the corner for a magnificent team-goal, a glowing reminder that this was a team game rather than just a one-man show.

But not for long. From a corner, Bernardo was left completely unmarked at the far post. As we would see as the competition progressed, he's not the worst with his head, and his header across goal was perfect for Haaland to leap and power the ball at goal. Blaswich made another fine save, but was powerless as Erling stretched to half-volley the rebound home. And still he wasn't finished as, when the keeper could only parry a fizzing low cross into his vicinity, another crisp half-volley sent the ball crashing into the net.

To the disappointment of the crowd, and for sure the man himself, Haaland was substituted a few minutes later, denying him the opportunity to become the first man to score six times in a Champions League game. As Pep said afterwards, 'If he achieves this milestone at 22, his life would be boring. Now he has a target to do it in the future.' Even so, in netting his fifth, he'd become City's all-time top seasonal goalscorer, his 39th strike taking him past Tommy Johnson's 1928/29 haul of 38. One record at a time, please.

In injury time, De Bruyne, absolutely outstanding throughout, struck a fierce yet perfectly placed 20-yarder into the top corner to complete the scoring and confirm that he too was back on top form. But of course, it was difficult for anyone to talk about anything other than our Number Nine, already approaching other-worldly status.

Once again, all his goals were one-touch finishes, the more notable being the two that came in the second half. On each occasion he moved rapidly to get his body into a position to strike the ball first time, even though it meant stretching and being slightly off balance. Many would have instead elected to take a touch and then attempt a more composed finish, but Haaland combines instinct with the knowledge that speed is of the essence. He'll miss a few sitters because of it, but the likelihood of the shot being saved or blocked by a defender is dramatically reduced. The player himself says, 'I didn't think, it was just doing it, just trying to get the ball in the back of the net. A lot of it is being quick in the mind and trying to do the right thing – a little bit of it is quality but a lot is in the head.'

The Guardian's Barney Ronay was again in colourful form: 'By the time his fifth hit the net on 57 minutes Haaland wasn't really celebrating, just laughing, a man drowning in honey. It is easy to forget, seeing only his size, his power and certainty, that he is still a slightly goofy 22-year-old, that he has never won a major trophy. City's entire system is still being re-geared to suit his skills. This has been the challenge on both sides, to transform the world's greatest one-liner into a novel.'

Pep was unusually tetchy with journalists afterwards, still niggled by the criticism after the first leg. 'With the selection, if we win I am right, if we lose I am wrong. But I have a lot of information even you don't have. I have more info than the Twitter guys. I am sorry. Today I am right. I am right.' His manner suggested a real irritation with pundits and journalists constantly questioning his selections, notably the exclusion of Kevin De Bruyne from time to time.

'Kevin is extraordinary, the rhythm he played today, his movement, is the Kevin we know ... and we haven't seen that so much this season … he is unstoppable,' said Pep. It was an interesting line, implicitly stating that the reason he's spent a few games on the bench is lack of form, rather than just being given a rest. 'What I'd like – I spoke many times to him – is to go to the easy principles and do it well. He has an incredible ability to make an assist, to score goals and see passes like no one else. But I always have the belief that he will get better when he does the simple things, like don't lose the ball.'

So here's to a couple of months of Kev doing the simple things. Who knows where it might take us.

19

18 March 2023, FA Cup:
City 6 Burnley 0

'If we play good, Erling will score goals'

THE FA Cup fifth-round draw throws up an away tie at Ashton Gate. We almost take the lead in the first minute, as the lesser-spotted Kalvin Phillips thumps a long-range drive against the bar, but only have to wait a few more minutes for Phil Foden to tap in at the far post after a typically incisive link-up between De Bruyne and Mahrez. It's a cracking 'old-fashioned' cup tie, with Nigel Pearson's team really going for it and their fans roaring them on against the Haaland-excepted full-strength glamour boys. It's like the cup used to be and it feels like, year by year, we're getting back to those days.

The home side come close to equalising on a few occasions but City get a second when Álvarez sets up Foden to sweep home via a deflection, and the tie is wrapped up when De Bruyne surges forward and bends a beautiful low 25-yarder into the far corner. It's a fabulous finish, and it says much for KDB that when he lined up the shot, everyone in the ground, everyone watching on telly, expected him to score.

So with most of the big teams out, two of them at the hands of City ourselves, we look well placed to return to Wembley, especially when the draw hands us a home tie against Championship opposition. But it's not just any Championship side – it's runaway leaders Burnley and, more to the point, their manager Vincent Kompany.

One of the most popular and influential players in the club's history, Vinny remains revered by City fans, his very own 'Here's to you, Vincent Kompany' chant still emanating regularly from the stands and getting regular airings on away trips. And we're all delighted to see him doing so well at Burnley, evidently with a style of play that's a breath of fresh air compared with the diet of muscular, functional football that's been their lot over recent years. 'It's like night and day,' says one of my Clarets-supporting pals, when comparing the Sean Dyche regime with what Kompany's side is now delivering. For sure, if they can keep this up and prosper when they return to the Premier League, Vinny will be the popular choice to replace Pep when he finally takes his leave, and Pep himself wouldn't argue with that, saying, 'I think his destiny to be the manager of Manchester City is already written in the stars.'

For now though, Vinny will get his first taste of life in the Etihad dugout as boss of the visiting side, although it certainly doesn't feel like it. He's introduced to the crowd, as if that was necessary, and accorded a rapturous reception, smiles and hugs with old colleagues everywhere. The mutual affection is there for all to see, and the feelgood mood continues as Mike Summerbee is presented to the crowd after receiving an OBE for his charitable work. Vinny gives him a hug as well, but then it's on with the baseball cap, off to the touchline and down to business.

Burnley acquit themselves well in the early stages, creating a couple of half-chances without coming really close, but with Haaland around good work can be undone in an instant. And after half an hour or so, that's exactly what happens. In a reprise of his second goal against Leipzig, he comes short to meet a clearance from Ortega, bringing the Burnley centre-backs up with him. As soon as he nods the ball back to Álvarez, he spins and sprints into the space he's opened up behind the defence. Álvarez slides a precise through ball between two defenders and Haaland races on to it, that startling pace enabling him to get to the ball before the onrushing Peacock-Farrell and prod it into the net.

Within a minute it's two, as De Bruyne sets Foden galloping down the left. A perfect low cross finds the onrushing Haaland, who opens up his body to clip the ball artfully across the keeper for his second goal. It really is Leipzig revisited, the similarity further enhanced in the second half when he pounces on the rebound after Foden's shot hits the post to bring up yet another hat-trick. And it's another of those finishes where he instinctively adjusts his body position to enable him to strike the ball first time, almost falling over backwards as he gives himself room to convert with a single sweep of his left foot. This aspect of his finishing technique really is something special, requiring a level of co-ordination scarcely credible for a man of his dimensions. It's as if he's got his own internal rule, that the goal will be disallowed if he takes more than one touch.

Pep quashes the chance of another five-goal salvo by bringing him off to yet another standing ovation, but there's precious little relief for Burnley as De Bruyne in particular is once again really in the mood. He drills in a low cross for Álvarez to tap home and, after Cole Palmer knocks in a close-range fifth, Kev produces the pass of the match, a beautifully weighted ball inside the defender for Álvarez to sprint on to. There's still a lot for him to do, but he cuts back inside expertly to create a yard of space before instantly thrashing a brutal shot past Peacock-Farrell. It's such an Agüero-like finish that you almost have to do a double-take to make sure it isn't really him.

But not for the first time, a moment of exceptional quality from Álvarez fades into the background. There's only one name on everyone's lips. Eight goals in four days; eight goals in 125 minutes of playing time. Not too shabby for a man supposedly playing for the wrong team. As usual Pep is asked to forecast how many goals Haaland might end up with; as usual he evades the question. 'This guy will have a problem in the future, every game he will be expected to score three or four goals and this is not going to happen. He doesn't care because he is so positive, so optimistic, he never complains. The numbers, I don't know. But if we play good, Erling will score goals.'

For Vinny, it's not quite been the return he'd hoped for, but his team have other priorities and even when they get promoted they won't face Haaland every week. He says, 'The biggest thing for me is his game can still improve and that is maybe the difference with the other superstars. To me he looks like a superstar who is willing to improve and that is exciting to see.' It's a relentless theme, almost as relentless as Haaland's goals. He's already at the top of the game, but all he wants to do is get better and better. With his age and his attitude, it's hard to imagine he won't. Where will it end?

It's been a fantastic couple of weeks for City and, after that tricky month or so, we seem to be properly back in the zone. But now it's the international break. It's bloody annoying, coming just when we've built up real momentum. I've never been that bothered about how England do, and

I never will be. You can't choose your country but you *can* choose your team. So what else can we do but have a nice breather and hope that everyone stays fit? And after that we'll have a possible ten weeks of two games a week, almost all of them a case of lose and you're out.

20

1 April 2023, Premier League: City 4 Liverpool 1

'He's the same Jack, but now he believes he belongs here'

SO HERE we are. The home straight, albeit a bloody long one. It's full steam ahead to the end of the season and, like all clubs, City are praying that no one comes back injured from their time away. With Erling still recovering from a minor injury picked up against Burnley we don't need any more bad news but, when Phil Foden is rushed to hospital with appendicitis, he's clearly set for a few weeks out. It's a big blow for City but even more so for Foden himself, who'd come back towards his best form after that difficult period. Phil at his best gives us something that none of our other players can provide, and there'll be occasions where that directness, drive and ingenuity will be sorely missed. And possibly none more so than in the next game, at home to Liverpool, against whom some of his best performances have come.

The first game after a break has often seen City struggle for rhythm, but it's preferable to have a fixture against another top team, who've had their routine similarly disrupted by a large number of international call-ups. Although, at least this season, Liverpool haven't looked much like a top team. Injuries to key forward players haven't helped, but with a midfield lacking mobility and an attack lacking Mané, they've often struggled to compensate for their defensive deficiencies, with Van Dijk showing nowhere near the authority of previous years and Trent frequently pilloried for his wayward defensive positioning.

The 9-0 against Bournemouth and 7-0 against United showed that they're still capable of battering the little teams, but their overall form has been well short of the standard set in the previous few years, epitomised by their capitulation against Real Madrid after taking an early 2-0 lead. Klopp himself has got plenty of credit in the bank, but openly admits that if it wasn't for past achievements he'd be under serious pressure. They arrive at the Etihad with just the faintest hope of reaching the Champions League slots, and to do so will require one of those formidable runs when the pressure's really on. But everyone knows what they're capable of, while we'll be without both Foden and Haaland. This won't be easy.

From the start City are on the front foot, Mahrez bending a free kick just wide, but then Liverpool escape the press and with Akanji and Dias looking to play him offside, Jota scampers off towards goal. Akanji does well to recover and hold him up, but Jota shields the ball for the onrushing Salah and with that all-too familiar sweep of his left foot, the Egyptian bends his shot past a helpless Ederson. It's the sort of counterattack goal that Pep hates to concede, and we can't blame this one on having Haaland in the team.

It's a jolt but City continue to create openings, a lovely move ending with Mahrez blazing just over, although when our next attack results in a corner it's time to get worried.

The fact is that Liverpool are more likely to score from one of our corners than we are. Sure enough, De Bruyne's delivery is headed clear, and when Stones misplaces his header, Salah is put through on the left, well clear of the trailing defenders, with Jota sprinting up to make himself available for a tap in. But as Salah plays the ball inside, it's intercepted by Jack Grealish, who's hurtled back at a speed never previously witnessed, to save City from going two goals down. It's exceptional work from Jack. His play with the ball has improved beyond recognition and here he shows that his off the ball awareness, his embracing of the team ethic, is also right up there.

Grealish is soon in his more familiar position, out wide on the left, and after a flowing move featuring outstanding play from each of De Bruyne, Mahrez and Gündoğan, he slides a perfect low ball across the face of goal, eagerly despatched by a jubilant Álvarez. It's a fabulous goal, one of the best team goals of the season, and further emphasises the importance of Jack's intervention a few minutes earlier. And, as he keeps warm in the comfort of his executive box, the cameras pick out the watching Erling Haaland, celebrating wildly in the style of a true fan. Which, of course, he is.

It's been an exhilarating first half which we've largely dominated, but the second is better still. Within a minute, another superb end-to-end goal has City in front, this time instigated by a clever reverse pass from Aké and followed by a glorious crossfield ball from Álvarez to Mahrez. A low first-time cross just evades Alisson and the onrushing De Bruyne taps the ball home. These are not the sort of goals we score too often these days, generally because our opponents' defensive formations preclude it. It's classic counterattacking football, made possible by Liverpool's high line – would they have set up this way had Haaland been playing? – but so beautiful to watch.

City now have Liverpool penned back, with Stones having moved forward, almost playing as a number eight. There's little space to play with in the final third but an intricate passing move, with Álvarez to the fore, ends with Mahrez again sliding a pass into the Argentinian. He gets a shot away but the ball is blocked by Trent, only for Gündoğan to take a touch before calmly planting it into the unguarded corner of the net.

Liverpool are being absolutely pummelled, but their threat on the transition remains very real and when Aké takes a heavy touch after intercepting a cross, Gakpo goes over his attempted tackle for what at first sight looks like a penalty. The well-placed referee waves the appeals away, and within seconds we're at the other end, Grealish hitting a curler which is tipped away by a full-stretch Alisson. Replays show that Gakpo had executed a blatant simulation, attempting to wrap his foot around Aké's calf in the style of Rodney Marsh some 50 years ago. Subtle it wasn't; punished it should have been.

And finally, perhaps the best goal of a very impressive lot. City manipulate the ball around the centre circle, a long sequence of passes eventually creating the space for Gündoğan to drill a diagonal ball out to Grealish on the left. De Bruyne tirelessly sprints outside him, taking the pass and immediately cutting a reverse ball into space inside the area. Jack fastens on to it and at full stretch slides the ball low past the keeper for a magnificent fourth, a goal which his performance richly merits.

And he's not alone in his excellence. Mahrez has been sensational, at his silky, sinuous best, while Stones has provided an adaptation of the role previously played by Rico

Lewis, stepping up unto midfield and sometimes beyond. He looks as though he was born to do it, so comfortable and composed on the ball, and Pep's not even slightly surprised: 'Always I thought he had the quality to play there, it's not really easy to play there. Alone would be difficult but alongside Rodri helps.'

Meanwhile, Álvarez has been a revelation, nominally replacing Haaland but frequently playing in a deeper role, heavily involved in the build-up and showing an impressive array of passing. And it certainly had more than a touch of the 'false nines' about it. Before Álvarez arrived at City, Tim Vickery, the South American football expert, described him as 'a striker with the soul of a midfielder'. And while he doesn't yet have the close control of a Bernardo or a Foden, he's certainly already adept at finding space for himself and getting his head up to see what's available. The turn and sweeping pass to free Riyad early in the second half was exquisite, as was the interplay in a tight space which led to Gundo's third.

And his pressing – particularly where he plays instead of Erling rather than alongside him – has always stood out, although today there was one slight aberration. And as he went into our jubilant dressing room after the game, Álvarez offered an apology to Pep and the coaches. He'd tried to press Alisson during the first half, rather than stay in position and block a passing lane, and Liverpool went up the other end to score the opening goal. But Julián's performance after that more than compensated.

Rivalling Álvarez for all-round excellence was Jack Grealish. As Sam Wallace observed in *The Independent*, 'His goal was only his first at the Etihad Stadium all season. It came in what was perhaps his best performance yet in a big game for City after 18 months at the club. A slow start in the big time for Grealish but now he feels fundamental to Guardiola. The skittering runs, the imperceptible changes of direction, the inevitable foul from the helpless defender – the Grealish effect is strong. You just will not see it expressed in the data.' A point with which Pep was in full agreement, 'Football is not just stats, look at the interception to deny 2-0. The way he gave us the right tempo to play and make the extra passes, I can't imagine the big name he is and the price the club paid, the humility to run like a teenager. That means a lot to me and the team. He's the same Jack, but now he believes he belongs here.'

Bernardo was also full of praise: 'Today he was unbelievable! Sometimes your first season at City is not easy. For me it wasn't, for Riyad Mahrez it was not easy as well. People just think that you're going to come into one of the best teams in the world and be the best player on the pitch every game. It just doesn't work that way. It's tough. The manager demands a lot from the players, it's a different style of play from most of the other teams, so you have to get used to it and now he's been here for quite a long time, he's used to it and he's doing well. When he's in this form it's really good for all of us.'

There's some talk in the studio that Rodri might have been given a second yellow card when he brushed against Elliot with the score at 1-1, and although the contact was slight you've certainly seen them given. But so battered were his team by the end that Klopp hardly referred to the incident afterwards. 'So 1-1 at half-time it's clear we have to defend; they had a massive overload and we don't even have a challenge! These things cannot happen but they happened, after that they could do what they want – we were lucky they were not in the most greedy mood. There is nothing good to say about this game … we cannot not have challenges in key areas, we cannot be that open, I cannot explain it, I can just describe it. I'm not sure we would have won against ten men.'

The April fixture list is littered with big games, vital games, but we absolutely couldn't have got off to a better start, with Pep calling it 'one of the best performances in these seven years'. And the journos are also suitably impressed. In *The Independent*, Richard Jolly called it 'a game of coruscating brilliance, the pace and drama illustrating why it has become English football's modern-day *Clásico*' while the *Daily Mail*'s Oliver Holt rang out a warning to Mikel Arteta. 'Put it this way: Arsenal had better hold their nerve at the top because City are coming. It is as if the gargantuan effort of the battle with City last season sapped Liverpool of the energy for the fight this time round.'

And that's a really good point. Pep may have questioned his own players' hunger after having won so much, but how much more difficult must it be to drag yourselves up again after the disappointment of coming so close but just missing out? Still, for City the hunger was back, and in spades. 'We know we lose a game, we lose the competition. It's a good way to play,' Pep admits. And from hereon in, it'll be the only way to play.

21

8 April 2023, Premier League: Southampton 1 City 4

'You're just a shit Rickie Lambert'

AFTER THE magnificent second half against Liverpool, we next faced a trip to Southampton, scene of one of the worst performances of the whole Guardiola regime three months earlier. But that felt a long time ago, in that post-Qatar phase where we didn't seem fully focused. Now, though, the mindset is very different.

Haaland is fit again but there's speculation in the press as to whether he'll start, with Álvarez having been so inspirational against Liverpool. But when it's a game you need to win, Haaland always starts. It's really tough on Álvarez, but he's not the only one to be relegated to the bench after producing an outstanding display. Mahrez in particular has suffered the same fate on a few occasions this season. It must be hard to take, and requires a special type of mentality to cope with it.

Southampton were in dire straits and dire form, bottom of the table and winless in their last four outings, and a similar game to the one at Selhurst Park was widely anticipated, with City having to be patient before ultimately wearing the opposition down. And that's exactly how the match panned out, as we played with typical composure but failed to convert a handful of decent opportunities.

There was just one scare as, in another example of how our own corners are a major source of danger to ourselves, Mahrez attempted to cut the ball back to De Bruyne, some 25 yards out. Sulemana had anticipated the move, getting there in time to nick the ball off Kev's toes and haring unopposed towards our goal as Kev again declined to take a yellow for the team. Roy Keane would be appalled. Aké was closest in pursuit, and got close enough to his man to force a slight stumble as he bore down on Ederson, the keeper then managing to smother the ball.

All of City's threat was coming down the left side, with Grealish and De Bruyne combining frequently and to great effect, their interchanging and movement creating numerous crossing opportunities, and eventually, just before half-time, the breakthrough came when De Bruyne's curling cross was met by the unmarked Haaland, who leapt to plant his header home from close range. It was De Bruyne's 100th Premier League assist, for people who get excited about these things. I'm one of them.

If the first half had been hard work, the second was a stroll. Haaland dropped deep to pick up the ball and instantly fed De Bruyne, whose pass set Grealish away down the left. He was being forced on to his left foot, but rather than trying to cut inside as usual, he drilled a low left-footer which Bazunu did well to get down to. The rebound came straight back at Grealish who without breaking stride swept it home with the outside of his right foot.

It was a really smart finish and for Jack, an unusual one. Even his biggest detractors couldn't dispute that he was now living up to his price tag, and well worth his place in the starting 11. But although his end product had improved, it still seemed that every pass, every cross and particularly every shot was made with that same old sweeping arc of his right leg, curling the ball with the inside of his foot. Although this was increasingly delivering the goods in terms of passing and crossing, when it came to shooting his efforts were so predictable, always looking to bend the ball in at the far post. But here he showed, twice, that he could actually strike for goal in a different manner, and it paid off handsomely.

City were enjoying themselves now, and the De Bruyne-Grealish link-up down the left soon brought further reward. Jack took the ball on into the area before clipping a cross – inside of the right foot in-swinger, naturally – which was a little behind Haaland. No bother. Haaland stopped, leapt, flung his left foot into the air and from the corner of the six-yard box executed a perfect scissor kick across Bazunu for a quite stunning goal. The Zen pose was revisited as City fans behind exulted and even some of the home fans could be seen shaking their heads and applauding. 'You're just a shit Rickie Lambert,' they'd cried when Erling put a decent early chance wide – well, Rickie must've been one helluva striker.

With nothing to lose, Selles sent on substitutes Moussa Djenepo and Sékou Mara, and the two combined with a Djenepo beating three reluctant-to-tackle City defenders in a mazy dribble before squaring for Mara to fire home, but any suggestion of an unlikely comeback was quashed within less than a minute. De Bruyne raced through the middle after an intricate move only to be scythed down by Walker-Peters for the season's most clear-cut penalty. Still, a couple of the Saints players had the gall to dispute the decision, presumably more as a tactic to delay the kick rather than in any belief that their complaints were justified. With Haaland by now having been substituted, Álvarez stepped up to blast the ball confidently home and complete the scoring.

The talk afterwards, naturally, was mainly about Haaland and in particular his acrobatics for his second goal. 'It is not easy to pick the ball up in the sky and put it on the grass,' said Pep with commendable understatement, while a smiling De Bruyne said, 'You will never see me do that or you can get me to Southampton hospital.' And De Bruyne had plenty to smile about, a superb display confirming that he was back to his best, as we approach the time when we need him most. Pep tried to define what makes him unique. 'Kevin has that ability that is so hard to find, running at full speed and can still find the passes. Normally players have to run a bit slower to see the passes – when he runs slower he loses the ball.' And when you look back at his century of assists, so many of them have been delivered while he's been sprinting, yet somehow able to assimilate what's happening elsewhere. It's a very special talent.

And Pep really pushed the boat out in his praise of Haaland. 'As top scorers we lived two incredible decades with Cristiano Ronaldo and Lionel Messi but he is on that level.' It's a big claim, but in terms of pure goalscoring it's justifiable, certainly in terms of their records at this stage of their careers. 'Erling's just 22, he's arrived in the hardest league in the world – I can talk because I've been in other leagues – and he's here for these type of games.'

But equally heartening as the crux of the season approaches is the form of so many key players. Bernardo, whose cameo today was quite superb, can't even get a start. But you can bet he'll be restored for the Champions League games. In the past, it was one below-par performance and you'll be out next week. Now, as Álvarez discovered today, even an exceptional display isn't enough to guarantee your place next time round.

This is one of the arts of Guardiola's management, instilling that true squad mentality, everyone supporting everyone else, understanding that in a pool of elite performers not everyone can play every game. To be a successful part of this squad requires not just outstanding ability but also the mentality to understand that sometimes you'll be axed even when you've done nothing wrong. In fact, sometimes, even when you've done everything right.

Nine games to go, five points behind Arsenal and as the showdown with them at the Etihad draws nearer, we still need a two-point shift to put the title back in our own hands. 'I would like to be in the position Arsenal are in, I have to be honest,' says Pep, even though the bookies make us favourites, doubtless based on the been there, done that factor.

It's reached the stage where we're as familiar with Arsenal's remaining fixtures as we are with our own and the one which has stood out for weeks is their trip to Anfield. Despite Liverpool's underwhelming form this season, this is almost as difficult a fixture for Arsenal as it is for us – their record at Anfield is nearly as bad as ours, with no wins since 2012 and a few chastening pastings along the way. And with the home crowd surely at full throttle, will the young pretenders be able to stand up to it? For weeks it's been let's just worry about our own games and control what we can control, but now we're tuning in to their fixtures with a similar level of intensity.

The Sunday afternoon at Anfield starts badly, as Arsenal slice through the centre of the Liverpool defence in a manner which would have been unthinkable even last season. Martinelli prods the ball home to give his team the perfect start and things get even better for them, and worse for us, when Jesus is left criminally unmarked, just six yards out, to head easily past Alisson. Arsenal look irresistible, Anfield is flat, and we need something to happen.

And suddenly it does. Arsenal's old ability to self-destruct returns when Xhaka, so impressively and surprisingly mature this season but here showing that a leopard never completely loses its spots, gets involved in a spat with Alexander-Arnold. It enrages the Liverpool players and crucially the crowd as well, who almost as if by the flick of a switch are transformed instantly from sedate, almost stunned onlookers to actively hostile participants. Their team respond, Salah forcing home at the far post to set the game up perfectly for the second half.

And it's a second half as thrilling as anyone could wish to see, consisting mainly of Liverpool laying siege to the Arsenal goal. Salah misses a penalty, Ramsdale saves his side time and again, before with just three minutes to go, the soon-to-be-departing hero Bobby Firmino plants a header home. Liverpool pile forward in search of a winner – please lads, a draw suits us fine, don't do anything stupid – and almost get it but then deep into injury time Martinelli breaks away, with Saka completely in the clear, untracked. It's a real hide-behind-the-sofa moment. Please, not another added-time winner! Mercifully Martinelli overhits his pass and we can breathe again.

The final whistle blows. Objectively, it's a game that Liverpool deserved to win but a draw is all we needed. There are nine games left and – barring an unlikely shift in goal difference – if we win all of them we'll be champions. What a ridiculous sentence that once would have been. Since when could anyone talk about winning nine successive games in the hardest league in the world as if it's even possible, never mind probable, but this is the level we're at. It's still a huge ask, but it's not as if we haven't done it before.

It's been a really positive weekend. The lift Arsenal would have got from a win in their most daunting remaining fixture – coming after the highs of their previous two added-time victories – would have fuelled their momentum and belief still further. But suddenly, the juggernaut is sitting squarely in their rear-view mirror. I wonder whose position Pep would rather be in now?

22

11 April 2023, Champions League: City 3 Bayern Munich 0

'To knock out these teams you have to have two good games, not just one'

IF THE title race wasn't exciting enough, next up was a Champions League quarter-final against Bayern Munich. They're the German Manchester United. If you don't support them, then you hate them. Their hierarchy moan on and on about the unfairness of competing against clubs with mega-rich owners while year after year they themselves pick off whatever talent they fancy from their rivals. And for anyone who says our recent so-called dominance is bad for the game, how about the Bundesliga? Bayern have now won 11 consecutive titles, with all but two won by double-figure point margins. How is that healthy? They are truly a bastion of self-interest, and complete hypocrites to go with it.

It was generally thought to be the toughest draw City could have received, with the added disadvantage of being at home first. Worse still, the draw for the semis had already been made, and should we get through then the winners of Real Madrid and Chelsea would await. Real Madrid, who can do no wrong in this competition, or Chelsea, having a desperate season, but English. And our record against English opposition in Europe is as dismal as it gets, being eliminated every time. I'd definitely prefer to have another crack at Real, but that's getting ahead of ourselves. Bayern, for sure, will be more than a handful.

They arrive under new management, with Pep's occasional nemesis Thomas Tuchel at the helm. They also bring with them two former City players, or technically one former player and one current, in Leroy Sané and João Cancelo. Cancelo is eligible to play but finds himself on the bench, while Sané starts in an attack which also includes Kingsley Coman and Serge Gnabry. No shortage of pace there, and it feels a little surprising that Kyle Walker has been left on the bench. With Stones again set to be largely deployed as a holding midfielder, Aké and Akanji will face a good few one-on-one duels. For City, Bernardo predictably comes back into the line-up, replacing Riyad Mahrez.

Once again there's evidence that City fans have finally embraced this competition, the traditional jeering of the UEFA anthem followed by an almighty roar setting the tone for the raucous atmosphere to follow. It's the sort of thing that City routinely have to face on their travels and its value is brought home early on, as a jittery Sommer delays his clearance and the rampaging Haaland gets a touch on the ball but not quite enough to divert it into the goal. Haaland soon gets a more conventional opportunity, set up by Jack's clever flick, but strangely goes for a side-footer rather than putting the laces through it, and it's an easy save for Sommer. Wherever Erling goes, a stat follows. In seven previous meetings he's never won a game against Bayern Munich.

It was good to see Leroy receive a warm reception on his first return to the Etihad. The sight of him brings back fond memories of Pep's first title-winning team, the Centurions of 2017/18, when he played such a vital and frequently thrilling part in our success, in what seems those distant days when we attacked with two out-and-out conventional wingers. A left-footer on the left wing and a right-footer on the right. It'll come back into fashion one day, and people will call it revolutionary.

Leroy's ability was never in question but there were always doubts about whether his mentality and attitude would allow him to make the absolute most of what he had to offer. His shock exclusion from the Germans' 2018 World Cup squad certainly hinted at an attitude problem, and at City it ultimately seemed as though he wasn't best equipped to cope with the concept of not necessarily playing in all the big games. But he provided some fabulous memories and was essential to our successes. By all accounts his form at Bayern has been a bit in and out but we know full well what a threat he can provide. And tonight he looks in the mood, skipping past Akanji on the left then cutting a perfect ball back for Musiala. It's the best chance of the night so far but Dias makes himself as big an obstacle as possible and manages to make the block.

It's already a game of high quality, pace and intensity, and Bayern certainly haven't arrived here with any inferiority complex. But then, as we approach the half-hour mark, Bernardo slides a lovely little pass into Rodri, some 30 yards out. Rodri cuts inside his man, moving the ball on to his left foot. The ball sits perfectly for a shot although, while he's scored some spectacular long-range efforts, they've all been with the other foot. But here he sets out a curler outside the far post, using Kimmich as a shield, and it arcs perfectly back on target, just evading Sommer's fingertips as it crashes into the top corner. It's a wonderful goal, and sees us ahead at the interval after a pretty even first half.

Bayern's attacking efforts are focused primarily on getting Sané free down the left, and early in the second half he makes serious inroads, twice firing fierce drives at Ederson. The first is particularly vicious and bounces off Eddie's chest but the second is low to his left and forces him into a fabulous and vitally important save. It's end to end and tense and, if the crowd are getting jittery, the same can certainly be said of the Bayern defence, notably Dayot Upamecano, whose indecision in his own area provokes a Keystone Cops sequence of ricochets, almost gifting a goal to Haaland.

City build up some momentum as the half progresses, and Sommer is forced into excellent saves from both Aké and Dias, but the next chance comes courtesy of another Upamecano error. He dawdles on the ball and Grealish, in his tigerish 2023 mode, wrestles it off him before cutely back-heeling it into the path of Haaland. Haaland strides into the left side of the box and although everyone is baying for him to shoot, he's already taken a look up and instead floats over a delicate cross to the far post. Steaming in to meet it is Bernardo, who nuts it with all his might across Sommer, and the keeper's fingertips aren't strong enough to prevent it crashing into the net. It's a shocker from the Bayern defender, but the contributions of all three City players in the goal are outstanding. Haaland's awareness of the options available is particularly impressive, especially for a man so often lazily referred to as a goalscoring machine and nothing else.

Álvarez, on for De Bruyne, then forces a full-stretch save from Sommer as we sense the chance to take a complete grip on the tie. And a few minutes later we do,

Stones heading a Rodri cross across goal for the unmarked Haaland to expertly guide his volley home, with Upamecano inexplicably ball-watching. There's time for one more super save from Sommer, tipping Rodri's header over the bar, before the final whistle comes. It's a great result, could have been even better, but one we'll certainly settle for.

If Sane's return had been welcomed by the home fans – other than when he was bearing down on our goal and firing grenades at Ederson – the same couldn't be said for Cancelo's reception, roundly jeered when he came on as a late substitute. For sure there's been a major upturn in our form since his departure. There are rumours of training-ground bust-ups, and City fans' interpretation of everything they've heard is that Cancelo is the bad guy. You can't imagine him ever coming back, but it's a funny old game.

'For Manchester City to sail so serenely past the six-times European champions shows how far Pep Guardiola has already taken them,' said *The Guardian*'s Jamie Jackson, but it really only felt serene in the late stages of the game. Bayern had posed plenty of problems before then and Tuchel's observations afterwards weren't wholly unreasonable. 'I think it is not a deserved result, it does not tell the story of this match. We played with personality, courage and a lot of quality but we didn't get the rewards we deserved. This does not feel a 3-0 but it is a 3-0. It is a huge task to turn it around but we will not give up.'

Just eight days later and it's off to the Allianz Arena. Red hot favourites we may be – 'we've almost no chance' said Tuchel, as if anyone would take any notice of him – but Pep is having none of it. His challenge is to make sure that there's absolutely no complacency; in particular, an early goal for Bayern could change the complexion of the tie completely. After a flurry of meetings in our early Champions League years, we haven't played there for a while, and none of the City side had appeared there in our colours. But they should know that it's not a ground where you want to be giving the home side any encouragement.

Pep is certainly well aware that we can't take any liberties. 'It was an incredible result but I know a little bit what can happen in Munich. If you don't perform really well they are able to score one, two, three. To knock out these teams you have to have two good games, not just one.'

Aké had done well against Coman in the home leg, leaving Sané as the Germans' major threat, but in the early stages here it looked set to be a different story, with Coman sprinting clear early on to send in a cross only just beyond Choupo-Moting. But it was Sané who had Bayern's big chance, a quick break seeing him race clear only to clip the ball beyond Ederson's far post, leaving Pep on the touchline puffing out his cheeks in relief.

It was nothing to the relief his counterpart felt a few minutes later, as Haaland sped on to De Bruyne's pass to burst towards goal, only to be brought down by Upamecano. The red card was a formality, but the hapless defender was reprieved when replays showed Erling to have been narrowly offside. But the two of them would soon be the at centre of the action once again, when Upamecano deflected Gündoğan's shot with his arm, giving Haaland the chance to put the tie's outcome beyond doubt. It was fully three minutes before he could take the kick, with Bayern players first arguing with the referee and then indulging in distraction techniques, claiming the ball wasn't flush on the spot. Haaland's normal routine was interrupted and instead of striking low for a corner as he'd done with all his previous penalties, he went high down the middle, only succeeding in blazing the ball over the bar.

Erling just had to suck up the jeers and wait for the next opportunity, but he's proved to be quite good at that. A few minutes into the second half, an electric sprint saw him get on to the end of Grealish's cute pass only to shoot straight at Sommer, but his next intervention would settle the tie good and proper. After a narrow escape at the other end, Stones cleared and Haaland held off De Ligt to nod the ball back to De Bruyne. Erling was immediately on the move and Kev duly put him away, with just Upamecano to navigate. It hadn't been the happiest tie for the French defender and he soon suffered another mishap, stumbling and falling over. Erling calmly dinked the ball over his outstretched leg, before looking up and planting the ball high past Sommer. Haaland ran off to celebrate not with his usual evident jubilation, more with the demeanour of a man with his frustrations released. There was a real edge here. These are two sides that really don't like each other very much. It feels like a lot of it stems from Tuchel.

Bayern gained some late, inconsequential consolation with a penalty after Mané's cross was blocked at point-blank range by Akanji's arm, but despite the hopeless situation Tuchel continued with his ill-tempered protestations whenever a decision went against Bayern, and was eventually sent to the stands. Not an easy man to warm to. The final whistle soon confirmed an outstanding 4-1 aggregate win for City, who by now knew the identity of their semi-final opponents. Although they refused to be drawn into saying so explicitly, revenge would be very much on the agenda. But for the next few weeks, the focus returned wholly to domestic matters.

23

26 April 2023, Premier League:
City 4 Arsenal 1

'This was barely a contest.
It was an evisceration'

IN BETWEEN the two Bayern fixtures, City had faced Leicester at home. The visitors were in big trouble, with Dean Smith having just been appointed to replace Brendan Rodgers to try to save them from the drop. Plan A for City was definitely to get the job done early, bring off a few key players to keep them as fresh as possible and get ourselves ready for tougher challenges ahead.

And we execute the plan to perfection. Within 25 minutes we're 3-0 up, John Stones with another of his 20-yarders and a double from Haaland, the first from the spot, the second a lovely dinked finish after being sent clear by De Bruyne. At half-time the two goalscorers are substituted and a few minutes later Rodri joins them on the bench. Soon afterwards De Bruyne and Grealish are also given a bit of a rest and the match meanders to an inevitable conclusion.

Or does it? It seems like we've not really got much appetite for further goals, and Leicester simply don't look capable of scoring any at all. But then, as Ederson makes a routine save from an innocuous Souttar header, Phillips gets in his way, causing him to spill the ball. Iheanacho has an easy tap-in, but instead of this being mere consolation, the nerves set in and it's game on. Our rhythm has been completely disrupted by the raft of changes and the fact that we've long since declared at three, and Leicester are reinvigorated. Rúben's lazy pass out of defence is intercepted and Maddison sprints through, but Ederson spreads himself to make a vital block. Iheanacho is the next to find himself clear on Ederson, but his crisp effort strikes the inside of the post and comes out. The tension among the crowd is tangible but we hold on.

All's well that ends well, but it's a reminder for Pep of the risk of making too many substitutions. It's reminiscent of the home derby, when we allowed United to grasp the merest tinge of respectability with their two late goals. But at that stage we were 6-1 ahead. Evidently even three goals isn't a watertight lead these days, and it ended up being an extremely uncomfortable finish to the game. Kalvin Phillips, given almost 40 minutes to settle in and perform in a match seemingly already won, had a torrid time, and later confesses that this was a real low point, even in a season pretty much bereft of highs. 'I was rubbish. I went home and cried.'

The first season under Pep is often difficult, unless your name is Erling. But it's been even more so for Phillips. At least he tried to draw a line under the weight issue: 'For me, I wasn't overweight, but obviously the manager has seen it in a different way. I just took it and did my best to get as fit as possible. It was just one of those things, a misunderstanding between me and some staff members.' It's been such a tough start for Phillips that you wonder whether he'll stay beyond the summer. Whether he'll even want to stay beyond the summer.

His failure to bed in properly hasn't cost us, at least as yet, as Rodri has been exceptional, growing in stature year by year. And despite having played more minutes than anyone, you feel that you'd have to drag him off the pitch, especially at this stage of the season. And he sums up the mindset which every member of the squad has locked into. 'The difference between being champions or not is these months, so we have to be the best version of ourselves. The mentality, the leadership has to be there. I've been here four years and you see the faces of the lads ... every time we get to these moments there is less laughing, more focus and seriousness. The only thing you can do is win, win, win, win. There is no time to draw. Sometimes it is tiring because it seems like you can never have a day off but this is what you have to do. I assure you that if we want to win this Premier League we have to win every game. I see the level of Arsenal and they have just one competition to focus on and we have three. They can prepare for every game like a final and rest and we cannot so we have to win every game.'

But will Arsenal buckle under the pressure? Rodri adds, 'When you've done it before you have proved that you can do it again. If you've never done it, maybe you have doubts over whether you can.' And, based on the events of the last couple of weeks, those doubts are really starting to surface at the Emirates, if not among the players then certainly their supporters. After their draw at Anfield, Arsenal had again been held in their next game, away at West Ham. And again they had given up a two-goal lead in the process. Then, in their next game, they almost unimaginably found themselves 3-1 down at home to relegation certainties Southampton. They roused themselves, equalising close to the end, and with eight minutes of added time to play looked set to find another late winner. But somehow the Saints held out, sentencing Arteta's men to three straight draws – and putting us in the box seat for the title, five points behind them but with two games in hand.

And so, as the long-anticipated top two shoot-out was finally upon us, it had a very different context. For so long it seemed that City would have to win just to keep in touch, with the fixture also serving as an insurance policy for Arsenal. If they'd slipped up elsewhere, they could always get themselves back on top by winning at the Etihad. But now that they actually had slipped up, they needed to cash the policy in.

A win for Arsenal would put them back in control with just five games to play; a win for City would allow us the luxury of one slip in our last seven games. For either side there'd still be a lot to do, but the psychological impact of the result – especially for Arsenal – would be vital. Win at City and all the frustration and disappointment of the previous three games would be banished and their self-belief fully restored; lose, and despite whatever messages of defiance they might put out, it would be hard to see them coming back.

There'd been talk in the media of the Arsenal wheels coming off, which just goes to show how absurdly high the standard is: they hadn't actually lost a game since we beat them at the Emirates ten weeks earlier. And Pep was having none of it: 'Playing them at this stage of the season was always going to be difficult, but after three games dropping points, it will be much more difficult. I would have preferred it if they had come here with better results.' The backlash factor is always a worry. And for City fans, Arsenal's comeback to get a 3-3 draw against Southampton brought back memories of 2012, when Mancini's men similarly scored two very late goals to earn a point at home to lowly Sunderland. At the time the result felt like a disaster; in the end, the point earned with that late fightback won us the title.

So would Arsenal persist with their core tactics of an aggressive high press supplemented with tight man-to-man marking? Within that, there would still need to be lots of tactical nuances, as Arteta explained prior to the game, 'The issue with a team like City is that it starts with the goalkeeper and he is a threat when the ball is with him. You have to control every single one. They can do so many things. They play with a box inside, they can play with a diamond, they can build the game with three, they can be asymmetric on one side, they can play Bernardo on the right and play with a diamond with Kyle Walker higher. You have to be adaptable to take the game where you want it.'

Their biggest challenge would be keeping Haaland quiet. But how? Kolo Touré had a foot in both camps, having been a stalwart of Arsenal's 2004 Invincibles before moving to City, where his most memorable and lasting contribution was to feature in one of our most famous chants, joining forces with his rather more influential little brother. Though they're gone, the chant lives on, primarily by way of well-lubricated spectators at the World Darts Championship, which is about as incongruous as it gets. Still, I suppose it's some sort of tribute to our ingenuity; after all you never hear the Ally Pally throngs sing 'knick-knack paddywhack, give the dog a bone' do you? But then what person with a mental age greater than three would want to sing that?

Kolo had one 'must-do' piece of advice, and it didn't seem like rocket science. 'He's very quick and very strong, so you cannot get too tight to him, because he can roll you. You have to make sure you have at least one metre between you.' But would Arsenal's central defenders heed his words?

This was a night which had been anticipated for months, and the atmosphere fully reflected it. We wouldn't want for encouragement and within just two minutes the crowd were even more fired up, as Ramsdale could only parry a low cross from Grealish into the path of De Bruyne. As Kev pulled his foot back to shoot, he and Thomas Partey collapsed in a tangle of legs, but Michael Oliver ruled that De Bruyne had fouled Partey rather than the other way round. It was the sort of challenge you could watch back hundreds of times and not be clear as to who'd fouled whom, and a narrow escape for Arsenal.

Their relief wouldn't last long. Within five minutes, with the visitors pressing aggressively as expected, John Stones launched a long ball towards Erling Haaland, situated in the centre circle with Rob Holding at his back. Controlling the ball with a featherlight touch, Haaland turned the defender and immediately released the already sprinting De Bruyne. With space to run at the defence, Kev eased the ball on to his right foot and, from almost 25 yards, side-footed an exquisite daisy cutter into the corner of the net.

This was a magnificent goal, Haaland's touch under the severest pressure from Holding was supreme, and as for De Bruyne's finish – first impressions were that Ramsdale should surely have done better with a shot from that range, but the sheer precision, starting the ball outside the right-hand post so that it came back in only after it had bypassed the keeper's fingertips, made this the harshest of judgments. Maybe Holding could have done with taking Kolo's advice, as he'd gone touch-tight to Haaland but was nowhere near strong enough to knock him off balance, before being left stranded by Erling's perfect control.

It was fair reward for an all-guns-blazing start by City and a taste of what was to come from Haaland and De Bruyne. Arsenal may have felt that they'd pressured us into playing long, but the move for the goal looked well-rehearsed, with Stones playing the ball precisely into Haaland's feet and De Bruyne on the move as soon as he did so. There was clearly a plan in place, bypassing the press not just by playing the ball to Haaland but also employing De Bruyne in a more advanced role to play off him. The two of them soon combined again, Haaland coming short to receive a pass through the lines and immediately prodding it through to De Bruyne, already on his travels towards goal. This was a role reversal that Arsenal simply couldn't cope with, but Kev didn't quite have the pace to break free and Ben White managed to get a block on his shot to keep his team afloat.

Their next combination was more conventional, De Bruyne sending Haaland away. Some magical footwork saw him cut between two Arsenal defenders but Ramsdale just managed to fingertip his shot away. Haaland let out a roar of agonised frustration, but Arsenal were being cut to ribbons. After Ramsdale had repelled his ferocious angled volley, some beautiful interplay between De Bruyne and Grealish set Haaland on the rampage once again. Weaving one way then the other against defenders terrified to commit themselves, he eased the ball on to his left foot and as his shot passed the keeper most of the home fans were already on their feet to celebrate. But the ball passed literally an inch outside the post, leaving Pep and thousands of others with head in hands. Still the chances kept coming, Ramsdale again denying the striker from close range after great work from Gündoğan.

Haaland was unplayable, next holding off Partey with ease and drawing a foul. De Bruyne's delivery to the far post saw Stones make an early run and plant a header across Ramsdale from the corner of the six-yard box, only for an immediate offside flag to curtail any celebrations. It looked like the correct call to the naked eye, but as the VAR check went on and on, optimism rose that Stones had somehow managed to stay onside. A few sporadic cheers emerged from the stands, as those in touch with folks watching on TV at home got the news that the goal was legal – how can it be right that armchair viewers know what's happening before fans inside the ground? – and Michael Oliver soon confirmed the good news. At last we'd got a second goal, even if it represented a mere fraction of what our dominance had deserved.

Could Arteta formulate a half-time plan if not to turn the tables then at least to stem the tide? Evidently not, as Haaland soon turned Holding with ease to surge towards goal once again. The speed of this guy from a standing start is astonishing – it looked as though Arsenal had plenty of covering defenders, but he simply burned away from them only for Ramsdale to deny him yet again by way of an outstretched leg. But no matter if his finishing hadn't quite been on the mark, he had his role as a creator to fall back on. And when De Bruyne nicked a ball through to him after a mistake from Ødegaard, he played his part to perfection, delaying his return pass until Kev was in the optimal position. He calmly stroked the ball through Holding's legs and beyond Ramsdale to make the game safe.

Holding extracted the merest recompense from his night of suffering with a smart finish after City had eased off slightly but the last word went to Haaland, who finally got his name on the scoresheet after Foden's cute control and clever pass set him free to slot past Ramsdale. It was fitting reward for the striker's best all-round performance of what was already an extraordinary season and it crowned a magnificent display from City, who'd come up with a plan to exploit Arsenal's tactics and executed it superbly. If the defeat was damaging enough for Arteta's already wounded side, the manner of it had surely have battered their morale to a point where recovery would be impossible. Arteta conceded that Arsenal would need to win all five of their remaining games to have even the slightest chance and if he could galvanise his team to achieve that after the mauling they'd taken this evening, it would be a feat of management bordering on the miraculous.

According to *The Guardian*'s David Hytner, 'It was a night when Erling Haaland was frightening to watch from the press box so goodness knows what it was like for Holding and Gabriel in the centre of the Arsenal defence. There were times when he seemed to bulldoze through, when it actually felt unfair,' while the BBC's Phil McNulty was similarly impressed. 'Haaland was not quite at his ruthless best in front of goal but there were other qualities to admire, qualities he has acquired since the start of the season, fashioned by Guardiola and taken on board by a player with almost frightening room for improvement. The striker was relentless, worked tirelessly and showed a mastery of build-up play and ability to bring others into the game that was a revelation.'

In the *Daily Mail*, Oliver Holt's take was, 'This was barely a contest. It was an evisceration. It was a humiliation. It was a lesson. It was the most formidable statement of intent any team has made in the Premier League this season,' while Patrick Vieira, another with a foot in both camps, said, 'This was a statement from City to say, "You're still a long way from us." It was a strong performance and City showed they are going to go on and win it.' And win it was what everyone now expected City to do, with *The Sun*'s Dave Kidd claiming, 'The Gunners find themselves leading the Premier League in the final week of April but with approximately zero chance of winning it.'

As for Mikel Arteta, there was none of the 'we made it easy for them' bollocks which had followed our win at the Emirates. 'We were beaten by the better team, that's for sure ... they were exceptional today ... you have to accept we have lost against an exceptional team, and that's the level.' And, between the lines, a level which he knew his team were not yet capable of matching. So how had we come to dominate them so comprehensively after two tightly contested meetings? The magnificent De Bruyne offered some insight.

'The way that Arsenal press the opposition is top,' he said. 'It is class. Honestly, it is really, really good and it is almost impossible to play from the back. We knew we had to play longer today and we tried a couple of things in training. I tried to get a little bit deep and then run off Erling when he kept the ball. We found that a couple of times and in the first half we created some chances this way. It was important to set the tone.'

City had lined up with İlkay Gündoğan playing in a deeper role alongside Rodri, allowing Kev to play with more freedom in attack. When Xhaka or Partey tried to squeeze up the pitch, De Bruyne would loiter in the area vacated, explaining, 'I had the freedom to go left or right depending on where the space was. I had to choose the moments, depending on who pressed out of Xhaka and Partey. If Partey was pressing I would try to go on his back and the opposite way round.'

Meanwhile, as usual, the wide players created gaps in the middle of the pitch by holding their width. Pep's teams have always featured wingers, whether conventional or inverted, and the build-up phase requires them to hug the touchlines. Apart from providing a direct threat when circumstances permit, this has the obvious advantage of giving the central players more space to play in. And tonight that was the main benefit. It may have seemed that Bernardo and Grealish had a quiet time, being man marked whenever they received the ball, but by staying wide and drawing the full-backs out with them, the space they helped create for what at times looked like a front two was absolutely essential. And so De Bruyne and Haaland frequently found themselves in a two on two situation against Holding and Gabriel, and their movement and interplay did the rest, pulling one or even both of them into areas they didn't want to go.

Another tactical triumph was the role played by John Stones, and, for this, Pep acknowledged his debt to a player who hadn't even made it on to the pitch. 'It's thanks to Rico – he helped us to understand what we had to do to play better. The last ten games he didn't play much but without Rico this season, the step we made as a team would have been more difficult. I'm pretty convinced about that. The movement he does makes many things fluid. After that John Stones playing in that position has been exceptional.' Basically, Rico had been the prototype for the role that Stones was now making his own, demonstrating how the position helped support our build-up while protecting against central counterattacks.

* * *

Whenever Kev has a blinder against Arsenal, and it's happened a good few times, the pundit made to squirm most uneasily in his seat is Paul Merson. When City signed De Bruyne in 2015, Merson was scathingly critical, dismissing the player after his brief and unhappy stay at Chelsea a couple of years earlier. The brevity and unhappiness were both attributable to being managed by José Mourinho, by this time enjoying a final hurrah before embarking on his bitter, vindictive journey towards becoming a specialist in failure, raging against the dying of the light.

After leaving Chelsea, De Bruyne had scored 16 goals and provided 28 assists to help Wolfsburg to a second-placed finish in the Bundesliga and a victory in the German Cup. He was voted Bundesliga Player of the Year in 2015. This is not a league full of muppets. You've probably got to be quite good to get that. And yet Merson seemed oblivious to the progress De Bruyne had made.

Merson was asked if José Mourinho was wrong to let De Bruyne leave Chelsea for Wolfsburg back in 2014. 'I didn't think so. I didn't think he'd done it at Chelsea, he didn't get loads of chances but he didn't look part of the Chelsea way,' he replied. More accurately, De Bruyne didn't look part of the Mourinho way. So when City shelled out £50m to bring Kev back to England, Merson was flabbergasted. 'I just don't see this. I don't see £50m for this player.' And his colleague Phil Thompson was certainly in accord. 'De Bruyne? Honestly, the world has gone mad. You look at the amount of money they're paying for this boy. Absolutely bonkers. He's a good player, but is he a great player? Come on.'

De Bruyne wasn't overly critical when these comments were put to him some years later, but by then his performances had spoken eloquently for themselves. 'Obviously, I think a lot was said when I signed for City and the amount of money,' he said. 'And at that moment in time when a lot of articles or people would say something, I had the feeling, "People don't watch other leagues."' And that, shamefully for pundits employed to give 'expert opinion' on football and footballers, is the crux of it. For most of them, nothing but the Premier League matters – or even exists. Once Kev had left Chelsea he was instantly branded a failure and his rapid progress elsewhere was totally off the radar.

Well, they may not watch the German league but they certainly watch this one, and general consensus nowadays is that Kevin De Bruyne is one of the greatest – if not the greatest – attacking midfielder ever to play in it. To be fair to Merson, it's a fact he's fully acknowledged on numerous occasions. And tonight was one of Kev's finest performances of all.

24

6 May 2023, Premier League:
City 2 Leeds United 1

'You have to take it!'

'THAT MENTALITY where you have no option but to win is the best mentality to play' was another of Pep's mantras, and City were now properly in the zone, locking into ruthless mode when it really mattered, with the Arsenal game making it seven successive league wins.

We now faced three league games in a week, all eminently winnable, and here was the chance to put our foot on Arsenal's throat before resuming the assault on the Champions League. First up is a trip to Fulham, by far the Premier League's most enjoyable away ground to visit. Marco Silva's men have surpassed pretty much all expectations by sitting in the top half of the table but, with nothing tangible to play for, they surely represent the ideal sort of opposition at this stage in the season.

As I take my place in the stand behind the goal, there's a very familiar face in the seat directly in front of me. Not that I can actually see the face, but I don't need to. It's the A-side of a very recognisable back of the head. Noel Gallagher – a proper, knowledgeable City fan who would make a sight better pundit than most of those appointed to the role – is here, usually spotted in an executive box but today just another Blue. I get the sense that this is what he prefers – I hope so anyway – but the one downside is that he gets pestered by people wanting photos. Again and again and again. I've never featured in so many selfies in my life, as numerous City fans' souvenirs of a brief encounter with a Mancunian legend are marred by this grouchily contemptuous old geezer in the background. Can't you leave the poor bloke alone, he's just come to watch the footy with his mates!

Pep brings in Álvarez, in tandem with rather than instead of Haaland, while Kev is said to be not feeling too good and doesn't make the squad. He's certainly earned a rest. As usual, Álvarez impresses from the off. He's never played in Europe before, never mind England, yet he's settled in so quickly that he's already a key member of the squad, even though he doesn't benefit from getting the rhythm of regular starts. And he's already shown the versatility to play in different positions, a prized attribute in any Guardiola player. At just 22 years old, it's already looking like we've pulled off a serious coup, and how much better is he going to get?

Álvarez makes his mark very early, latching on to a Mahrez cut-back in the area only to be felled by a clumsy challenge from Tim Ream. Another clear-cut penalty, and Haaland banishes the memory of his aberration in Munich, returning to his preferred technique of sweeping the ball low into the corner. Every goal he scores these days seems to either equal or break some record or other – this is his 34th in the league, equalling the all-time Premier League record, and his 50th in all competitions, a feat not achieved since before the Second World War. We're completely on top but with their first incursion into our area Fulham get level when Harry Wilson nods the ball down for Vinícius to score. Vinícius scoring against City is definitely not an occurrence we want to see too often over the next couple of weeks.

We're soon on the front foot again, hounding Fulham into giving up the ball and instigating a move which sees Haaland cleverly set up Grealish on the left. Surprise, surprise, Jack goes for a side-footed curler into the far corner but Leno just gets enough on it to tip it on to the bar and away to safety. But shortly afterwards, some more excellent pressing, this time by Akanji, leads to the ball being threaded through to Álvarez, 25 yards out. He doubles back to create a yard of space and then strikes a wonderful dipping drive above and across Leno into the top corner of the net. Noel turns round and says to no one in particular, 'What a goal that was!' and there's no argument from any of us. It was an absolute screamer.

We start the second half looking to kill the game off, and some exquisite skill from Álvarez sets him up to play another of those sweeping crossfield passes that we saw against Liverpool. Grealish quickly squares to Haaland, whose instant shot brings a fantastic save from Leno, changing direction to tip the ball around the near post. Álvarez soon brings another top save from this excellent keeper but as the game reaches its final quarter the momentum shifts, with the physical and emotional energy expended in the Arsenal game taking its toll. A proper mix-up between Ederson and Dias almost gifts Decordova-Reid a goal, Ederson rescuing the situation with a desperate dive to claw the ball away from the striker's feet amid howls for a penalty.

The final few minutes see City indulge in blatant acts of time-wasting, bringing yellow cards for Ederson and

Walker, and the final whistle is received more with relief than elation. But at the end of a week like this, it's all about the result, and we're back on top of the table, a point clear with a game in hand.

'We tried to close certain areas of the pitch, not to give them a chance to play through our block,' Marco Silva said. 'But they have other ways to attract you on one side and to go to the opposite side and punish you.' And a crucial element was the double spearhead of Haaland and Álvarez, as a delighted Guardiola observed. 'The presence in the box with two guys is an incredible weapon that we have. It helps me a lot, especially in a tight game, against teams which play five at the back, it's so important for us.' Sounds like we haven't seen the last of them playing together, then.

Arsenal show some character the following day by beating Chelsea to go back to the top, sending the message that they haven't thrown in the towel just yet, so City take the field against West Ham three days on needing a win to return to the summit. David Moyes's team have had a dismal season in the league and are by no means safe. We all know what to expect from a Moyes team, and it sure as hell won't be pretty. And when West Ham are struck by a sickness bug before the match, Declan Rice among the casualties, it looks more certain than ever that survival mode will be their stance from the start.

City came close when Rodri side-footed against the post, but otherwise created little of note in a predictably frustrating first half. West Ham's approach, which Moyes would argue was borne of necessity, was nicely described by Phil McNulty in his BBC report: 'With Kurt Zouma ruled out through injury, it left Moyes to pursue a plan of containment and, as a backup plan, drop further back. When City had the ball, Michail Antonio moved to a position almost on the left of a midfield three. Behind that were two deep-lying midfielders and a five-man defence. It was almost as if West Ham needed a 12th player to give them an attacking option.'

The only question was whether the Hammers could hold out for a goalless draw, but their defensive discipline deserted them early in the second half when Riyad Mahrez hit a far-post free kick and Nathan Aké rose unchallenged to power home a header. The shackles were off and a few minutes later came the moment most of the crowd had been waiting for, as Grealish played Haaland through to chip the ball delicately over the advancing Fabiański for yet another record-breaking goal. Now, at the first time of asking, he'd broken the all-time Premier League goalscoring record, with five matches still to go. Phil Foden added a third with a superbly struck albeit heavily deflected volley, registering City's 1,000th goal under Guardiola in less than seven seasons. It's an extraordinary statistic, but once again the headlines belong to Haaland, receiving a guard of honour from his team-mates after the game, together with more brutal backslapping than any man should be made to endure. You're always going to love someone whose goals win you game after game, but you sense that this goes a lot deeper. There's a genuine affection for this guy. He might be a bona fide superstar at just 22, but he's still one of us.

As usual, he's very matter of fact in the post-match interviews: 'I'm going to sleep on this game and wake up tomorrow ... we will try to get three points against Leeds, it will not be easy with their new manager and everything. We cannot keep thinking about these records, I would become crazy in my head so I don't think of this. I will go home and play some video games and eat something and then sleep, then we think about Leeds. That is my life.'

And when we do think about Leeds, under normal circumstances it should be as straightforward a fixture as we could wish for. Our last three games against them have been won with an aggregate score of 14-1. But these are not normal circumstances. With just two clear days of rest between each of the last three games – and two more before our date in the Bernabéu – squad rotation is imperative. Dias, Walker, Stones, Rodri, Grealish and Bernardo, all certain starters against Madrid, are left on the bench.

It's a rare rest indeed for Rodri, but a chastening day for the man brought in to be his understudy, Kalvin Phillips. This was the most obvious opportunity so far for him to start a league game but Pep clearly still doesn't have the confidence in him, and his very sexy body remains seated on the bench. Instead, Gündoğan looks set to play a slightly deeper role, doubtless assisted by Rico Lewis.

For Leeds, there's precious little attention on the players selected, because pretty much all of it is focused on the new man at the helm. With just four games of their season remaining, their board have sacked Javi Gracia and taken the extraordinary decision to bring in their fourth manager of the season, Sam Allardyce. Big Sam has been out of football for two years, his most recent accomplishment being to lead West Brom to relegation in 2021. Since then he's been heard spouting his long-winded simplistic drivel on talkSPORT, but evidently this is the sort of thing their board think the Leeds players need in their desperate bid to avoid the drop.

In fairness, Sam had previously saved numerous clubs from relegation, apparently singlehandedly, before his stint at The Hawthorns, and also boasts a 100 per cent record as England manager, but the appointment smacks of something beyond desperation. I suppose if you think you're going down unless you make a change, what is there to lose? It does feel like a 100/1 long shot, but then so was Foinavon.

Still, if anyone thinks Sam's got the credentials to pull off a miracle, it's the man himself. 'I might be 68 and look old and antiquated but there's nobody ahead of me in football terms. Not Pep, not Klopp, not Arteta,' he said. 'It's all there with me. They do what they do and I do what I do. In terms of knowledge, I am not saying I'm better than them but I'm certainly as good as they are.'

Pep wasn't about to be drawn into any kind of headline-grabbing debate. 'He is right,' he said. 'It looks like the young managers invented football, but they did not. The old managers, look at what they have done. It will be tough to play Leeds because Sam has charisma and will pressure the players.' Pep may have very clear ideas as to how he wants his own teams to play, but he's never been heard to criticise managers who adopt a different footballing philosophy. Well, not in public, anyway.

Allardyce takes the decision to drop regular keeper Illan Meslier in favour of Joel Robles but City start as though the game will be done and dusted within half an hour. When Rico quickly puts Haaland through on Robles, the keeper gets his Premier League career off to a good start by saving with his legs. But it's just a matter of time, and the breakthrough comes inside 20 minutes. Mahrez cuts inside, rolls a cute ball to Gündoğan on the edge of the area and İlkay plants a sweet strike just inside the post. This really doesn't look like an Allardyce team. They're so timid, no pressure on the ball, almost just waiting for their fate to be confirmed. It's all well and good having 11 men behind the ball, but if they all stand around like statues the game becomes more like a training exercise.

After Haaland blazes just wide following another delightful move, Mahrez again cuts in from the right, again finds Gündoğan who again finds the corner of Robles's net. It's the other corner this time, and he even has the luxury of taking a touch before firing home. The five Leeds defenders between him and the goal all look at each other as if to say, 'Shouldn't you have tried to close him down?', not one of them taking the responsibility themselves. Meanwhile, chants of 'You're getting sacked in the morning' ring in Big Sam's ears, as City fans revel in taunting a man who apparently was offered the job of being our manager some 15 years ago. But then in came Thaksin Shinawatra and we went for Sven instead. Those were the days.

As unexpected bonuses go, Rico Lewis's emergence this season is right up there. Today he's playing more like a number eight than a hybrid right-back/holding midfielder, and doing it extremely well. He takes the ball on the turn, slides another lovely little pass through to Haaland on the edge of the box, and Big Erl swivels to strike a low shot which clips the outside of the post. He's having one of those days in front of goal, but it doesn't really matter. Or at least it shouldn't.

Despite all the possession, all the chances, we can't quite get that third goal to make the game totally safe, even though Leeds look as threatening as a fluffy pink unicorn with its horn cut off and teeth extracted. However, with six minutes left, Foden embarks on one of his thrilling incisive runs into the area before being sent tumbling by Struijk. It's been a frustrating day for Haaland, but here's the chance to further extend his record Premier League haul.

There's some confusion, with Erling having a bit of a chat with Gundo rather than beginning his usual penalty routine, and it suddenly becomes apparent that İlkay is going to take the kick himself. In recent weeks Haaland has shown himself to be increasingly unselfish, particularly noteworthy given that every goal he scores seems to bring up some sort of personal record, but this was taking it to a new dimension. This man who allegedly lives for goals was passing the opportunity away, in order to give Gündo the chance to complete his first ever professional hat-trick.

This of course is all well and good as long as you score. Gündoğan looks confident enough but his shot hits the post, rebounds back on to Robles and runs away to safety. Pep's not happy at all, storming to the touchline to point and yell accusingly at Haaland, 'You have to take it! You have to take it!'

Leeds have been absolutely hopeless, but a two-goal lead is never enough to start taking liberties, even against them. And sure enough, within a minute of Gundo's miss, they make a rare incursion towards the City area and a weak defensive header from Akanji allows Rodrigo to slide the ball past Ederson. From absolutely nowhere, Leeds have come from the brink of being 3-0 adrift to being right back in the game. It feels like a resurrection of Typical City. How can we possibly drop two points to a team like this?

But we don't. Despite the sudden influx of tension all around the stadium, City hold on in absolute comfort, even if it doesn't feel like it at the time. It's certainly unnecessarily stressful that we should finish a game where we've had 81 per cent possession trying to run the clock down. And so much for giving players such as Erling a bit of a rest ahead of the battles to come. Pep even resorts to an added-time substitution to eat up a few more seconds, with Rodri coming on to replace Gündoğan. There's no eye contact at the changeover, as our two-goal hero skulks off while Pep continues to glower. 'You're the bloody captain, you should have insisted that he took it!' is probably a polite interpretation of his thoughts. Nevertheless, it's a big three points – we're four ahead on equal games and Arsenal go to Newcastle tomorrow.

The main topic of conversation afterwards is Erling's selflessness and, after he'd calmed down, Pep gave his perspective. 'Always I have the feeling, when the game is 2-0, the main taker has to take the penalty. But that's how Erling is as a person. The top goalscorer, who has goals and goals, he gives it to his mate to make a hat-trick. I understand.' But somehow I don't think it'll be happening again.

Big Sam, as you'd expect, tries to take positives from the closeness of the scoreline – 'When you see Manchester City running down the clock for four minutes at the end, you know you have given yourself a chance' – but the truth is that Leeds were desperate, as poor as the sides who'd been here this season and hit for six or seven.

Allardyce also reveals that his pre-match boastful bluster was nothing but an ingenious psychological ploy. 'That's about taking the pressure off the players and putting all the focus on yourself,' he said, as if the thought of having all the focus on himself was completely abhorrent. 'The master taught me that – Fergie. He said you create a diversion, a stir. Say something to the press to take the attention away from players who are being criticised all the time. I went in there intending to say that. And, hey, I never said I was better than them.' I don't think many people are convinced.

So Arsenal head to Newcastle and if they don't win, it'll open up some serious daylight. I really think Newcastle will do it, and a blistering start sees them hit the post and have a penalty award overturned by VAR. Arsenal break out from under the cosh, nick a goal and from then on put on a highly accomplished display to come away with a 2-0 win. Fair play to them, that's a superb result and shows proper bottle. We're still red-hot favourites but three of our last four are away and all of them look tricky. In fact the more you look at them, the trickier they seem. It's always like that at this stage of the season. But we've now won ten league games in a row, only the tenth time that such a sequence has been achieved in the history of the Premier League. And City have been responsible for six of them.

25

9 May 2023, Champions League:
Real Madrid 1 City 1

'He just can't put a foot right at the moment'

BACK AT the Bernabéu. The scene of what even for those of us old enough to remember the dark, dark days, was perhaps the most gut-wrenching defeat in our history. The pain not just of having a place in the final so cruelly snatched away at the last, but then being left for almost a full hour to stew on what had just happened before being allowed out of the stadium. It's a memory burned on the brain. Barely a conversation could be heard as we struggled to come to terms with what we'd just witnessed.

At least this year the away leg is first, and there's no question about whether I'll be going back there. It's probably my favourite ground anywhere, absolutely majestic, banked so steeply that you feel you're almost on top of the action. And the sense of history is apparent both inside and outside the stadium. And I've come to love Madrid as a city – we've played Real so often that I've been to the Bernabéu more often than a lot of Premier League grounds.

With the other semi-final being the Milan derby, some pundits are saying that this is the real final. It may comprise the two competition favourites, but it's as if these people have never seen a Champions League Final in their lives. These games are not exactly littered with one-sided scorelines, even when that's the popular expectation prior to the match. But it's much too early to be thinking about that. The Bernabéu expects and we need to disappoint them.

Our start defines composure and confidence, keeping the ball, quietening the crowd and creating several half-chances. De Bruyne and then Rodri have fierce drives pushed away at full stretch by Courtois and, at the midway point of the half, City have enjoyed 72 per cent of possession. Seventy-two per cent possession in the Bernabéu. It's an impressive-sounding stat but it's nothing that Madrid and Ancelotti would be too surprised or concerned by. They have many strengths, but counterattacking and capitalising on turnovers are their most potent weapons. They almost score when a mistake by Rodri is seized on by Vinícius, but Dias makes an outstanding interception to deny Benzema a tap-in.

Then from nowhere, almost being penned in their own corner, Madrid spring out. Camavinga plays a lovely one-two with Modrić and steams away from Bernardo before slipping the ball to Vinícius. The winger's got space to run into and bears down on goal before, from 20 yards out, unleashing a fierce drive which flashes past Ederson to give them the lead. It's a brilliant goal, and when Pep describes teams as being 'amazing on transitions' this is what he means. It's also completely against the run of play, but we've seen Madrid do it so often that we know that's just a part of their strategy.

City don't panic and continue to look composed but when the second half begins we're put under sustained pressure for the first time. This phase of the game could be the crux of the tie and it's all hands to the pump as Madrid, finding energy from the crowd, win a sequence of corners. They're certainly the more threatening side, while if you had to pick one defender not to be intimidated by Haaland, to back himself to dominate physically, it would be Rüdiger. We still manufacture a couple of half-chances, Kev's angled drive being well saved by Courtois and Alaba pulling off a superb saving tackle when Haaland for once manages to escape Rüdiger's shackles. But our attacks are sporadic and at this stage most of us would settle for just a one-goal deficit ahead of the second leg.

De Bruyne's having one of those games, seeing enough of the ball to create some damage but his radar's off, with a sequence of misplaced passes. 'He just can't put a foot right at the moment,' I say to the guy next to me, but as usual Kev never hides, always wants the ball, always believes that his next contribution can make a difference.

And that next contribution comes ten seconds after I've ventured my typically less-than-expert opinion. A loose pass is intercepted by Rodri, and via Grealish and Gündoğan the ball is laid back to De Bruyne, in almost the identical spot from which Vinícius struck the opener. Without hesitation Kev puts his foot through the ball. It's a brutal hit, bringing his foot across the ball to impart the slightest swerve, but it's the sheer power which beats Courtois, who barely has time to blink before the ball crashes into the net. It's the sweetest of strikes, never rising more than a foot off the ground and as hard as I've ever seen him hit a ball.

As Kev and his team-mates head to the corner to celebrate, the Real players are up in arms, complaining to anyone they can get their hands on, and it's hard to see what their beef is. Nevertheless, as we all know in VAR World, you can never relax until they've kicked off. Those days of spontaneous uninhibited goal celebrations are a distant memory. Eventually, after Ancelotti is yellow-carded for his protracted protests, the game restarts, as we continue to wonder what had upset them so much.

Madrid rouse themselves for a final push, with Ederson making two excellent saves from Benzema and Tchouaméni, but City look increasingly happy to go back to the Etihad all square. It feels like a good result for us, though the reaction of Madrid's players and manager, as well as the Spanish press, is that it remains a 50-50 tie. Maybe so. And it becomes clear that the home side's protests related to the ball allegedly being out of play for a Real throw-in in the build-up to our goal. Watching back on TV, it does look as though it might have been out before Bernardo hooked it back in, but crucially Real Madrid then had uncontested possession of the ball before Camavinga gave it away to set up the phase of play from which we scored. Clutching at straws doesn't even come close.

It says much that a lot of people expected us to win comfortably here, and in some quarters there's a sense of disappointment with the result, but let's get realistic. An away draw at the defending champions in the first leg of a semi-final – you'd take that every time. Pep resisted any temptation to make substitutions, even when we looked to be struggling, and after the game he explained why. 'We have on the bench Foden, Mahrez, Álvarez. If you put one of them on in the Bernabéu at this moment, perhaps you will be more aggressive. Perhaps you will make a goal. But perhaps you will be less in control, and the goal is for Real Madrid.' Not defensive, just pragmatic. We've been outstanding at home this season, so let's make it a one-match tie. Pep the great innovator has adopted the old school two-legged European tie philosophy. You don't always have to be different.

26

14 May 2023, Premier League: Everton 0 City 3

'He turns into prime Zidane in the last few months of the season'

FROM THE moment we got through to the Champions League semis, this was the league fixture that stood out as the one to be wary of. Slotted in between the two Madrid ties, the last thing you want is an away match at a side battling relegation managed by a man who'll give them every encouragement to get seriously stuck in. But that's what we've got, and it's fraught with danger. It feels like a pivotal afternoon. A win for us will also be a crushing blow to Arsenal's morale, as their game doesn't start until after ours has finished. If we can get three points here, when there's so much noise about the Real Madrid tie, then are we really likely to slip up anywhere else?

There was a time, in the days of David Moyes and Tim Cahill, that this was a nightmare fixture for us. More recently, even though Everton have retained the capacity to pull off surprise results against leading teams, we've managed to navigate our trips to Goodison pretty well, winning on each of our last six visits. And Pep's record against Shaun

Dyche teams is extraordinary. Played 15, won 14, drawn 1, scored 46, conceded six. Yet it's the one draw which contained the most memorable incident, with Raheem Sterling's scarcely believable balls-up to deny us a 2-0 lead pretty much at the top of the list of his greatest misses.

So while Dyche may have the reputation of producing in-your-face sides difficult to play against, it hasn't worked too well against us in the past, and we certainly need to continue that trend today. Everton may be fighting against relegation but their last game saw them record an extraordinary result at Brighton, their 5-1 win being one of the shock results of the season. We don't want any more of that, thank you very much.

Given what lies ahead in just three days' time, Pep inevitably rotates, with De Bruyne, Grealish, Stones and Bernardo left on the bench. The game starts as expected, tight and cagey, and despite our usual territorial domination, there's not much threat to the Everton goal. We can't get Erling into the game and it takes 26 minutes for him to even get a touch of the ball. We've seen that before and it isn't necessarily the best news for the opposition. But it's Everton who have the first clear chance, Mason Holgate narrowly failing to turn the ball in following a set piece. They're not going to get many opportunities, but if they put one of them away then this place will erupt.

As we approach half-time the pattern of play remains the same, as we probe for the breakthrough against obdurate opponents happy to sit deep and defend in numbers. We've seen this match so many times before. We usually win it. Usually but not always. Then Riyad Mahrez gets the ball on the corner of the area, cuts back on to his left foot and spots a route through to Gündoğan, stationed near the penalty spot. Riyad clips the ball in, waist high, and Gundo controls it expertly on his thigh before, back to goal, executing the most audacious flick with his right foot, and the ball beats Pickford's dive to nestle snugly in the corner of the net. It's a beautiful, inventive finish and one for sure that was 100 per cent intentional, with Gündoğan having already taken stock of his position and knowing exactly where the net was. And of course it's an absolutely vital breakthrough.

Conceding just before half-time is deflating enough for the home team and their fans, but City capitalise on the situation by immediately launching an attack down the left. Gundo gets free and crosses perfectly for the soaring Haaland to nod past Pickford from close range. He almost headed it at him rather than past him, but the keeper couldn't change direction quickly enough to keep it out. So, what a few minutes ago was looking like a long hard slog now has a sense of inevitability – and perhaps might even give us a chance to protect a few more key players ahead of Madrid.

That would require a third goal, and just five minutes into the second half we get it. Another of Foden's incisive runs sees him cynically taken out just outside the area. Gündoğan's free kick is perfection, clipped over the wall and sailing into the top corner, and it's game over. For the second week running he's hit two goals, two outstanding goals, in a critically important game. What a footballer this guy is.

We see out time in comfort, and the afternoon couldn't have gone any better. No injuries, three points and a rest for plenty of key players ahead of Wednesday's blockbuster. And there's no doubt as to where the man of the match award is going.

'The £21m spent seven years ago on Gündoğan is one of those investments that stands comparison with any of the great buys of the Premier League era,' says the *Daily Telegraph*, and it's hard to argue with that. And his sudden goalscoring spurt comes as no surprise to Kyle Walker. 'I've been joking with Gundo that he turns into prime Zidane in the last few months. Sometimes you have to shine, and he always does it at the business end of the season.'

Haaland's goals may not have been not quite so plentiful in recent weeks, but there's no doubt as to the value he brings by his sheer presence. In *The Times*: Paul Joyce noted that Gundo had credited Erling for his sudden burst of productivity, saying the space he'd found in recent weeks is because defenders are always mindful of his team-mate. 'That, however, is typical of the German. A selfless, humble performer who makes those around him better but who can also sprinkle stardust, as he showed. If he is to leave in the summer upon the expiry of his contract, then he should be feted as one of the greats.'

Back in the centre of Liverpool after the game, Lindsey and I decide to take a couple of hours out to allow the trains back to Manchester to become less crowded. We find a nice tapas bar but I'm far less interested in the menu than I am in keeping up to date with what's happening at the Emirates. We're already very much in pole position, needing five points at most from our last three games, but it'd be lovely to have some insurance. I don't expect Arsenal to slip, but Brighton have been so impressive this season and Arteta's men must surely feel a little deflated after seeing our result, the sheer relentlessness of win after win after win grinding them down. This is when, as Klopp likes to put it, your players need to be mentality monsters – are this young side, unfamiliar with the extreme pressure at the end of the season, up to it?

The answer is emphatic. Brighton take the lead early in the second half and it sounds as though the belief has drained away from Arteta's players. The glances at the phone become more frequent and more anxious but when the news arrives that Brighton have added a late second, pretty well everyone else in the restaurant knows about it. An even later third makes it a horrible day for Arsenal and Arteta apologises to the fans afterwards. He's got nothing to apologise for. His players have never experienced this sort of pressure before, never faced an opponent capable of squeezing the life out of your hopes. Brighton are bloody good but part of the credit for their win today belongs to us. Week after week, Arsenal have lived in hope that we'll show some sign of weakness, that the door might be left slightly ajar, but every time we've slammed it shut. It can't be easy to keep on believing.

We're left in the position that if we win our next game, at home to Chelsea, we'll be crowned champions there and then. Worst case is that we'll need one win from our last three games. Three shots at the title. But how much better would it be if we took it at the first attempt?

27

17 May 2023, Champions League: City 4 Real Madrid 0

'For one year we have this
in our stomachs'

HERE WE go. They're saying that this is the biggest ever game at the Etihad. And if the biggest club game you can host is a Champions League semi-final, then it probably is. It's our third, but the first was a first leg and therefore not decisive and the second was played in Covid times. This time, the stadium's full and the world is watching. The atmosphere is quite something. We really have taken Pep's message to heart. After years of battling against intimidating crowds away from home, we're starting to give our rivals a taste of their own medicine when they come to the Etihad. It's taken a while, but we've got there and it's seriously impressive. We're all in this together. There's no more indifference.

In the days before the game, Real are still talking the talk, and with their record they've got every right to do so. But we're a frightening proposition at home, and so far this season we've stepped up every time it's mattered. United, Liverpool, Arsenal, Bayern – all put to the sword with majestic performances.

But in the back of everyone's minds, always, is the identity of the opposition and their capacity for winning this trophy in the most unlikely of scenarios. Not least last season, when it wasn't just against us that they produced something jaw-dropping en route to their 14th European Cup. Trailing 2-0 on aggregate against PSG with half an hour of the second leg remaining, a Benzema hat-trick saw them through. Then, after a comfortable win at Stamford Bridge, they found themselves 3-0 behind at the Bernabéu, needing a late goal to force extra time when, once again, Benzema struck the decisive blow. And after their miraculous escape against us, the final saw them generally outplayed by Liverpool but due mainly to a stunning performance from Courtois, they held on to take the trophy. Could any other team have come through four rounds in each of which, in every respect other than the one that really matters, they were the inferior side?

Interestingly, Ancelotti elects to bring Militão back, at the expense of Rüdiger. I'm delighted, and suspect Haaland is too. I'd expected them both to play but maybe that would have been seen as an admission of fear. They're too big a name to come here and try to contain. If he could have his time again, I wonder if Ancelotti would put his ego aside and adopt a more cautious approach?

From the start, City are fantastic. You can't really say anything else. Everything is on point. We're on a mission. And yet, after 20 minutes of brilliant, intense, inventive attacking play, of recovering the ball almost instantly whenever it's lost, the game is still goalless. Within the first few minutes Haaland rounds Courtois but is forced wide and no one can get on the end of his cut-back, then Rodri storms into the box but screws his shot wide. Haaland has two great headed chances, the first when a perfect Grealish cross sets up a sitter which he heads straight at Courtois when there's plenty of room either side, the second when he powers what looks like a perfectly directed effort back across him only for the keeper to almost miraculously get his fingertips to it and turn it around the post. If we had time to think about it, we might start to worry that it's going to be one of those nights. But there's none of that. The pace is so relentless, the determination and self-belief so self evident, the quality of football so jaw-dropping, that everyone's just living in the moment, roaring the team on.

Real, European champions, the undisputed all-time kings of Europe, just can't get out. Vinícius has scarcely had a kick, Benzema's almost an irrelevance, Modrić given no time to exert any creative influence, hounded into giving the ball away as soon as he receives it. The brilliance of Courtois is all that's kept them afloat but midway through the half even he's left helpless. A slick passage of play leaves De Bruyne 30 yards out, with space and time to pick a pass. Bernardo makes a clever run into the box and Kev slides the ball through. Bernardo takes a step inside, shapes to shoot towards the far post but instead whips the ball high into the near corner. It's a great move, a sublime finish and sparks scenes of delirium on and off the pitch.

At last we take a breath, and Madrid finally get a bit of possession in our half. Toni Kroos picks up a loose ball 25 yards out and lashes a fearsome drive which clears Ederson's fingertips and crashes against the bar. There's a sense of shock in the stadium. It's almost as if he'd scored. Never can we have been so dominant, and yet within an instant, out of nowhere, they were almost level. If we needed a reminder of how fragile a lead is, especially when playing against this team, the great escapologists, here it was.

But the warning is well-heeded. Some twinkle-toed trickery from Bernardo, as so often revelling in the big occasion; culminates in an instant shot on the turn from Haaland which flashes narrowly past the post, but City's next attack of note brings overdue reward. It features two increasingly familiar facets of our recent play, Grealish cutting in from the left, teasing a defender and waiting for an option to arrive. When it does, it's in the form of Gündoğan, making one of those late, unchecked runs into the area. Jack slides the ball in, Gundo takes it into his stride but his shot is blocked by Militão. The ball balloons up into the air, and waiting for it is Bernardo, 12 yards out. He's got time to assess the situation, and carefully plants a perfectly placed header above the covering defenders and into the net.

It's magnificent football, but no one needs reminding that two goals are not enough, and there's no sitting back. We continue to push for more, Pep turning to the crowd, urging them to ramp up the noise even further, and half-chances come and go before the half-time whistle blows. It's been an epic performance, as good as we can play, as good as anyone could play, but it's not over yet.

The second half begins with Real pressing a bit higher and for a time City are unable to recapture their rhythm. Alaba's long-range free kick is tipped over by Ederson. There's a snappy exchange between De Bruyne and Guardiola, reflecting the anxiety, the pressure, the knowledge that we're still in a game. Madrid seldom really threaten, but then they hadn't threatened much in the Bernabéu last season but still scored two in a minute. And every single City fan in this ground is all too aware of that.

We're less fluent in attack but far from hanging on. The defensive contribution of Bernardo is almost taken for granted but the efforts of Grealish are equally impressive.

Every facet of his game has taken a quantum leap since the World Cup and even his biggest doubters (and I suppose I must have been one of them) can't deny that he now truly belongs in this team.

As Madrid attempt to push forward, City create more chances to finish them off, the best of them arising from a fabulous intricate one-two between Haaland and Gündoğan. Gundo backheels the ball into Erling's path, but he can't quite get it out from under his feet and his shot deflects off Courtois's shin on to the top of the bar. Haaland hasn't scored but they haven't been able to handle him at all.

And then, at last, comes the breathing space. De Bruyne fizzes a free kick into the near post, Akanji gets the slightest touch and the ball deflects off Militão into the net. Ancelotti frantically makes the VAR signal, presumably hoping for an offside call, but after a short pause the referee confirms the validity of the goal and now, surely, even Madrid can't come back from this. The crowd certainly think so as, for the first time tonight, the Poznan is unleashed.

De Bruyne, visibly exhausted, finally gives way with a few minutes to go, to be replaced by Foden. Even in a minor cameo role, Foden still makes a big impression, taking a pass on the half-turn and instantly sliding a gorgeous reverse ball between two defenders into the path of the onrushing Álvarez. As Courtois comes hurtling out to meet him, Álvarez calmly slides the ball into the far corner for a goal euphorically greeted by the fans. The sprinkles on the cherry on the icing on the cake, and a scoreline that at least approaches being a fair reflection of City's dominance.

It's been one the greatest team performances, but it's hard to look past Bernardo Silva as the man of the match. I've yet to meet a City fan who doesn't love Bernardo. We first encountered him in his Monaco days, when he took the breath away with his display in an epic first leg, City won that game 5-3 but many of the overriding memories of the night were provided by Monaco players. Mbappé and Falcao were as scary as it comes but the real star was Bernardo, bossing midfield with his skill and boundless energy, seemingly everywhere at once. And Pep was certainly impressed, signing him up in the following close-season in what was another outstanding piece of business. When we get it right, we really get it right.

Bernardo's been heavily linked with an exit to warmer climes in both the last two summers, but we've managed to keep him here, and based on what he shows on the pitch he certainly doesn't look like a man who wants to leave. He's the template for a Guardiola player, totally committed to the team, intelligent, humble, supremely skilful yet a real competitor, and so versatile that he's played all across the front five positions and also had spells in deeper roles. As Jonathan Northcroft puts it in *The Times*, 'Silva is a remarkable player, a mini Swiss army knife, able to play multiple positions and perform numerous functions.' And he's evidently much loved by everyone at the club. He's produced so many epic performances over the years, his unquenchable energy and spirit often galvanising the team into achieving vital wins, but seldom has he been more influential than tonight.

'My performance in the first game in Madrid was not the one I wanted and I wanted to compensate that' Bernardo told BT Sport. 'Today I had to do better for my team-mates and the fans and that is what I tried to do.' And who would have bet that this little bundle of energy would score headed goals against both Munich and Madrid? 'I am small but good with my head!' he said with a smile.

Pep had refused to talk about revenge prior to the tie, but now it was over the truth came out. 'When the draw was Madrid I said, "Yeah, I want it." Last year had hurt, not just the defeat but the unfair reaction to it. These players being criticised, people saying that they didn't have character, when we lose because it's football.' And he'd sensed that something special was in the offing tonight, 'I had a feeling in these last days we had the right mix of calm and tension. You could smell the team was ready to perform at this level. For one year we have had this pain in our stomachs.'

Only that brief spell at the start of the second half prevented it being a performance of absolute perfection. Pep said, 'Right after the break İlkay lost a ball, Kevin made three transitions that weren't necessary and we rushed a lot when we had to do the opposite.' And those who thought the spat with De Bruyne was an issue were soon put right. 'The action with Kevin, I love it. We shout at each other. I like this from Kevin. Sometimes it's a little bit flat, I like this energy. It's not the first time, you don't see it, but he shouts at me in training. This is what we need of him. After that he becomes the best.'

And tonight, the whole team was the best, a fact that no one in the media attempted to deny.

The Times: 'This utter annihilation of Real felt like the moment when City more than avenged last year's semi-final loss. This was the moment when they truly looked the real deal, when they looked ready finally to become champions of Europe.'

Daily Mail: 'Manchester City, the club that existed for so long in the shadow of Manchester United, are dethroning the aristocrats of European football one by one and establishing a new order.'

Daily Telegraph: 'They were simply majestic. They were unstoppable. They were serenity delivered with a ferocious intensity.'

BBC Sport: 'Pep Guardiola is football's great perfectionist but even he would struggle to find fault with the night of sheer mastery produced by Manchester City to obliterate holders Real Madrid to reach the Champions League Final.'

Rio Ferdinand, BT Sport: 'They've battered, destroyed, pulverised a giant of European football. And they look like they've done it with ease.'

Thierry Henry, CBS Sports: 'Everyone knows I'm an Arsenal fan, but if you don't like City you surely have a problem in your head.'

It's been one of the very greatest nights, and when we finally leave the stadium there are fans around us still shaking their heads in wonder. It really doesn't get much better than this. Istanbul, we are coming.

28

21 May 2023, Premier League: City 1 Chelsea 0

'Having money is one thing. Investing it wisely is another'

THE WEEKEND starts here, but everyone still has a warm glow after Wednesday. It took me back to when we battered Schalke 5-1 in 1970, in the semi-final second leg of the Cup Winners' Cup. Schalke were no Real Madrid, but they were still a top team and, with them holding a 1–0 lead from the first leg, the tie was reckoned to be too close to call. Instead, we produced a display which caused their manager to describe it as 'football from another planet', and Malcolm Allison to hail as his greatest night. I can still remember that night more than 50 years later. I wonder if this one will be similarly cemented in the minds of our younger fans half a century on. It certainly deserves to be.

Back then, with City also-rans in the league, all the focus was on the final in Vienna a couple of weeks later. But this year's final is something for what seems like the distant future. There are other priorities to deal with first. To start with there's a Premier League title to be won. And one win from three will do it.

The first of the three is also our final home game. It's against Chelsea, whose season's gone from bad to worse since sacking Graham Potter, and the return of Frank Lampard certainly hasn't helped. In terrible form and with absolutely nothing to play for, they should constitute pretty much ideal opposition, but then didn't we say that about Villa last year? And Lampard showed when he brought his Everton team here that he knows how to spoil, frustrate and irritate.

But it might just be that we don't even need to worry about what Lampard and his army of expensive dysfunctional misfits might have in store for us. The day before the Chelsea game, Arsenal are away at Nottingham Forest. If they lose there, the title will be ours before we even take the field. There's a debate among City fans about whether that's what we'd prefer to happen. It's always more satisfying, more memorable, more emotional to actually win it on the pitch. On the other hand, after the weeks of stress, of final after final, knowing that the slightest slip could be terminal, how nice would it be to go to a match completely relaxed with no pressure and actually enjoy it from the start? I'm definitely in the camp of getting it over and done with at the first opportunity. There are more than enough forthcoming dates with the potential to create special memories. Come on, Forest!

Forest's need for the points is paramount – win and they'll stay up. They take an early lead and by the sound of it Arsenal aren't creating too many chances to get back on terms. As the game approaches its climax I find myself in the BBC studios at Media City. I sometimes indulge in a spot of performance poetry – which in my case essentially involves standing behind a microphone and swearing at people – and I'll shortly be taking part in a show put together by one of my spoken word pals. We've been invited in to talk about it on Radio Manchester's *Upload* show, hosted by a chap called David Scott. He's a rabid Red but also a great supporter and promoter of local creatives, so we can forgive him his misguided affiliation. We have a really enjoyable chat but I naturally have one eye on my iPhone screen throughout. We're into the last few minutes of added time and Arsenal are still behind.

But then it's my turn to perform a piece. I need to concentrate as I don't really want to balls it up live on air. As soon as I finish I look down at my screen to see that the '1-0' scoreline has turned black, with the word 'finished' beneath it. We've done it! David's also aware of the fact and also that I'm a Blue – the sky blue crest on my jacket was a bit of a giveaway – and he sportingly asks if I'd like to announce the news to the listeners. So it is that I get to deliver the glad tidings to the listening Greater Manchester public, or at least that part of it discerning enough to prefer a bit of local wordsmithery to the banality of early Saturday evening TV. I sound like an overexcited asthmatic – well, I am an overexcited asthmatic so what else would you expect? – but manage to achieve a degree of coherence as I report, 'Arsenal's 1-0 defeat at Nottingham Forest means that for the third year in succession and the fifth time in six years, Manchester City are Premier League Champions … thank you.'

Out of the studio, there's time for a quick drink before I head back to the pub, where the celebrations are in full swing. And judging from the state of Lindsey and our friends, they've evidently been in progress for some considerable time. I've got some serious catching up to do, but I give it my best shot.

By the time Lindsey and I make our way to the Etihad the following afternoon we're still a bit tired and emotional.

And at the moment the final whistle blew at the City Ground, the provisional team sheet for this afternoon's game was completely ripped up. Pep seizes the opportunity to give players a rest, and there are starts for Cole Palmer, Rico Lewis, Sergio Gómez, Kalvin Phillips and Stefan Ortega, All nine of our listed substitutes would almost certainly have started the game had it not been for Forest's victory. Palmer shines in the early stages and sets up Julián Álvarez to put us ahead, while Chelsea's best chances all fall to Raheem Sterling, who reminds us what we've been missing by fluffing the lot.

It's a carefree, low-key occasion, with everyone just waiting for the presentation and party after the match. The final whistle prompts familiar scenes, with the crowd, despite being told to stay off the pitch, streaming between the stewards to get on there. I could understand it if we'd just won the title, like last year, when the excitement's high and the adrenalin's coursing, but we've known for a whole day that we're champions so really, what's the point?

The medals are presented by Richard Masters, chief executive of the Premier League. The very same Premier League which has charged us with 115 breaches of financial rules. As Henry Winter puts it in *The Times*, 'After Real, the surreal,' also observing, 'However meaningless as a contest, this fixture against Chelsea was still fitting. It proved that having money is one thing, and investing it wisely is another.'

The player interviews are the same old, same old, as they all just want to get back to the celebrations, although there's a memorable moment when Jack's interview is interrupted by a jubilant Erling Haaland, screaming, 'I fucking love you man, you know that!' to his pal, prompting the usual apology to Sky Sports viewers.

All the tunes that have been appropriated for chants get an airing, some of them specially recorded with the adapted words already incorporated – minus expletives naturally – and it's all good fun, dare I say, as ever. With two weeks before the next meaningful match – albeit seriously meaningful – we assume that Pep will allow the players to let their hair down a little, and they certainly appear hell-bent on doing just that. And there's no doubt as to who'll be leading them.

Grealish is naturally exuberant in his interview and makes no secret of the fact that he'll be going out later to party. And his friendship with Erling has generated even more interest, and a perhaps a little concern. But it doesn't sound like Erling is the sort of person likely to be led astray. Jack had talked about it in a *Daily Mail* interview a few weeks earlier. 'Erling is the best professional I have ever seen. His mindset is something you won't see again. He does everything. Recovers. In the gym. Ten hours of treatment a day. Ice baths. Diet. That's why he is what he is. But I swear I couldn't be like that. We have a great friendship but he will point at me after a game and say, "Hey. Don't you go out tonight partying." I just tell him to shut up and go and sit in his ice bath.

'The main thing now is I feel loved. I feel the manager really trusts me. This is what I dreamed of. To play in every game for such an important team at such an important time. I am not gonna sit here and lie and say I don't go out. What's the point? It's also pointless telling you I am here at 8am going in the gym and that's the reason I am playing well. It's not. The reason I am playing well is because I feel fit, confident, good in myself and like I am at home here.'

* * *

The next big game is the small matter of a Manchester derby FA Cup Final. Both sides now have two weeks to prepare for the match, United having achieved their goal of a top-four finish, while our two tricky fixtures at Brighton and Brentford, for weeks eyed up with a degree of trepidation, are now just opportunities to rotate players, trying to keep everyone fresh while still in some sort of rhythm.

The game at Brighton is wonderfully entertaining, especially in the first half where Phil Foden in particular is outstanding, doing everything he can to stake his claim for a starting slot in the big games to come. Brighton really are a great team to watch but we take the lead when Haaland unselfishly frees Foden to squeeze the ball home. Brighton's equaliser is a stunner, the lively Enciso picking the ball up almost 30 yards out and unleashing a fabulous strike, curving into the top corner to leave Ortega helpless. It's one of those 'in as soon as it left his boot' jobs, as the camera angle from behind the player illustrates perfectly. City fans behind the goal are seen applauding the effort even before it actually hits the net.

The second half isn't quite so action-packed and there's more disappointment for Foden as he's subbed off early, apparently with a minor injury. The game eventually peters out but it's been a good, competitive fixture. And there's no doubt that our next outing will deliver more of the same, as we visit the bus stop in Hounslow, with Brentford looking to complete what for them would be a famous double. It's my first visit to their new stadium, and I like it a lot, small, atmospheric and with the fans really close to the pitch. It's a lovely sunny day and there's a real party feel about the occasion. Brentford are celebrating their best ever season, and us – well, these days it seems like we're always celebrating something or other.

Foden's recovered from the Brighton game and starts again, and he's much the liveliest of our attackers. Brentford take the lead late on and although we have glorious chances to equalise, Cole Palmer twice fluffing his lines from extremely close range, they hold out for a rapturously received win. Our long unbeaten run comes to an end, but if you're going to lose best to do so in a game that doesn't really matter. There's some talk about a loss of momentum, but is losing a game that doesn't really matter very different from winning a game that doesn't really matter? For more than a week, everyone's attention has been focused on the two forthcoming finals and now, at last, they're here.

He's one of our own — and king of the no-look finish

The spirit of Sergio lives on — another Alvarez screamer

That's just not normal – Erling puts his old pals to the sword

Where the hell did he come from? Varane and De Gea have no answer

Rico the record-breaker makes history against Sevilla

Kev at the Bernabeu – not bad for a man who can't put a foot right

Don't try that with me, son ... Kyle gives Vinicius ten years and five yards

I'm small but good with my head ... Bernardo slays the reigning champions

It's behind you ... De Gea wonders whether they've kicked off yet

Wembley men of the match – Silky Ilkay and Johnny Stones

When time stood still – Istanbul, 10 June 2023, 11.28pm

Calmness personified – Pep reacts philosophically to Phil's big missed chance

The most important save he'll ever make? City's last touch of the season

Reacquainted at last – Pep and Big Ears bridge a twelve-year gap

Now just you make sure you don't overdo the celebrations …

… suit yourself then. Beers are not enough for Hi-Viz Jack

29

3 June 2023, FA Cup Final: City 2 Manchester United 1

'Gundo saved me'

WHEN SOLLY March blazed his penalty over the bar in Brighton's semi-final shoot-out against United, I went into a proper hissy fit. It was the first miss after 12 successful attempts, and Lindelöf buried the next kick to send United to the final. Brighton had been so much the better team, their superiority progressively increasing as the match went on, that the outcome was a travesty. But to the delight of the TV hype merchants it set up the first all-Manchester FA Cup Final.

City had made their way there with what turned out to be a routine semi-final win over Sheffield United. We'd made our exit at this stage in each of the previous three seasons, every time fielding a less than full-strength side, our Champions League quarter-final ties providing a major distraction. On those occasions our Wembley opponents had been Arsenal, Chelsea and Liverpool, but this time the balls came out in our favour, with Sheffield United definitely the team we were hoping to get. Disappointingly for fans of both sides, City loanees James McAtee and Tommy Doyle were ineligible to play, a strange inconsistency given that João Cancelo had featured for Bayern in the recent Champions League tie.

Roared on by a full quota of fans, United got off to a strong start, having a great chance to take an early lead when Ndiaye's close range attempt was blocked by Ortega. But City's superior quality gradually came to the fore although it took a soft penalty, given for a foul on Bernardo, to give Riyad the chance to open the scoring from the spot.

The second half was increasingly comfortable, Mahrez scoring again when he sliced through the centre of the Blades' defence to slot calmly past Foderingham, before the Algerian completed his hat-trick, the first in a semi-final for 65 years, with a crisp finish from a Grealish pass. So now we have to wait a day to find who we'll meet in the final and, tough proposition as Brighton would be, there can't be a City fan who doesn't hope that they get through. But United scrape past them, and the inevitable bluster begins.

My immediate reaction is that they can stuff it, I'm not going. And this is even before confirmation comes through of the train strikes which will make the occasion even more insufferable. All I can think of is the absolute misery when they beat us through some diabolical VAR decision, sending the army of pathetic, bitter #stopthetreble merchants into orgasmic delight in front of their laptop screens.

Fortunately, I stop short of promising my ticket to someone else and after a week or so I come to my senses. This is a unique occasion, the sort of thing I'd spent decades imagining what it would be like, and here I am thinking I'm not going to go just in case we lose? Get a fucking grip! Yes, we'll have to mix with the moronic unwashed hordes before the game, but afterwards the two sets of fans will be leaving the stadium a good hour apart. Win or lose, there'll be minimal interaction.

The night before the final I'm up in London for a party. A gender reveal party. What is the world coming to? It's Tom and Maggie again. Is there any point? By the time the child reaches puberty, the burgeoning super-trendy, ultra-woke, Bandwagon Billy lynch mob will have shaped the world to the point where it really won't matter how you started out, you'll be able to describe yourself as whatever you like. But it's an excuse for them to get their friends together and drink far too much. There's lots of footy chat, and if anything more of it's about the following week's final in Istanbul rather than tomorrow's Greater Manchester derby. And that's good, because tomorrow's game is something I'm trying hard to keep out of my mind.

Tom doesn't have the history to be able to get a Champions League ticket via the club, and is weighing up whether to splash out on a ticket from a 'hospitality' outfit – or basically a scalper. He asks me for advice. Not a great strategy at the best of times, but after a skinful positively senseless. It's our second final in three years. Chances are there'll be others. But if we win at Wembley tomorrow, it'll be a game where we can win the Treble. Chances are that'll never happen again. It'll be a once-in-a-lifetime experience. It's only money. If you can afford it, go for it. But he's a bright lad, he knew what I was going to say before I said it. At least it'll give him someone to blame.

At the end of United's final league game, Ten Hag addressed the crowd after the final whistle. It had the feel of a far-right political rally, the atmosphere threatening and sinister. 'We will do everything to beat City and bring the cup back,' said the rabble-rousing Dutchman, prompting obligatory chants of 'United! United!' from the obedient wide-eyed drooling simpletons in attendance. You'd call them brainwashed if that had been an option. In most cases even washed would be too much to hope for. Ten Hag's choice of words was interesting. Beat City, rather than win the cup. Stopping the Treble comes first. They're more desperate to prevent us doing it than we are to win it.

Wayne Rooney also confirmed that priority. 'They have the chance to stop Manchester City winning the Treble and doing that would be huge. The unique status of the 1999 Treble forms part of the club's sense of pride and United players and fans absolutely won't want to rely on Inter Milan to preserve it.'

We set off bright and early, getting to the ground well before the 1pm gate opening time. The team is exactly as expected, Foden's recent excellence not quite sufficient to displace any of what's become Pep's preferred big-game 11. And that's simultaneously tough on Phil and yet fair enough, because who could you possibly drop? That grumbling appendix has cost him dear. Showing no respect at all for the fact that we're still living in Ferguson's lifetime, the bookies make us the hottest of favourites – we're quoted at 1/2 on while United are 5/1. It's the first time since 1951 that the crowd's been asked to sing 'God Save The King', and it's understandable that some people get the lyrics wrong. Though most of us don't sing at all.

City kick off with Gündoğan playing the ball back to Stefan Ortega. Nice gesture, letting the keeper get an early touch to help calm the nerves. But there's a bit more to it than that. With Pep there usually is. Ortega drills a long ball deep toward Haaland, who beats Casemiro to flick the ball on. Lindelöf heads clear, but the ball deflects slightly off the top of De Bruyne's head and doesn't get the distance the defender had hoped for. The ball loops up in the air, straight into the path of the oncoming Gündoğan. From 24 yards out, the skipper strikes a volley with a touch of fade and a ton of dip, which leaves De Gea completely static as it hits the back of the net.

It's just incredible. Twelve seconds. TWELVE SECONDS. City fans exult, United players are shellshocked, their game plan shattered in less than the time it takes the average United fan to recite the alphabet, though I suppose that would also have applied to a last-minute winner. But we mustn't get carried away. In my mind forever will be the 1974 World Cup Final, the Netherlands getting a first minute penalty without the Germans having touched the ball. Brian Glanville described the goal as a 'poisoned chalice', causing the already super-confident Dutch to think they had one hand on the trophy. Part of me still thinks that scoring so early could be the worst thing to happen, especially against them. If they equalise, the shift in mood from their current state of shock to the euphoria of getting back on terms could trigger a change in momentum difficult to resist.

On the other hand, if we can build on the lead before their heads have cleared we could be out of sight, and for the next half an hour that looks by far the more likely outcome. They can barely get into our half, but we can't find that crucial second breakthrough. Rodri's superb header from the edge of the area leaves De Gea just as static as he was for Gündoğan's opener, but the ball brushes the side netting on the wrong side of the post. What's becoming an increasingly common sight – Haaland dropping off, dragging defenders with him, laying the ball back and spinning to sprint into the space behind – almost delivers the goods. Gündoğan's chip over the defence looks perfect, but the full-stretch striker can only connect with his studs and the ball dribbles tamely into De Gea's hands. De Bruyne creates the space for a shot and even though it's not his cleanest strike it's still close enough for De Gea to go full stretch.

We reach the half-hour mark still just the one goal up, but not having been even slightly discomforted, apart from Manu Akanji, who's the victim of what looks like a deliberate over-the-ball stamp on his ankle from Casemiro. Disgracefully, the incident isn't reviewed by the VAR team. But then, Fernandes floats a diagonal ball across to the right and Wan-Bissaka runs beyond Grealish to head the ball across goal. The ball is cleared easily but United players are all asking for a penalty. There was no obvious contact but as play develops innocuously my eyes are fixed on the referee, praying that he's not going to halt proceedings. Some 30 seconds go by and just as I'm starting think everything must be OK, the whistle blows and even before he makes the dreaded VAR sign I know what's coming next. And sure enough, it does.

City players, especially Grealish, who's deemed to have handled, are distraught and plead their case, but as ever this is a futile exercise other than giving Fernandes more time to think about the task ahead. His stuttering run has the desired effect, causing Ortega to commit himself and allowing him to roll the ball in the opposite direction. From nowhere, having created absolutely nothing, they're level.

But that's not enough for Fernandes. One of the basic differences between the sides, their ethos, their culture, their mentality, is the way they celebrate scoring a goal. City celebrate with pure joy, delighted for the scorer and what it means for the team. But United so often look to take it one step further. Fernandes has got to rub our noses in it. He comes across towards the City fans in the corner, cupping his hand to his ear and yelling 'Vamos!' directly at them, mocking and taunting. Of course you're going to celebrate scoring in a cup final but you can do it without goading the opposition fans. Gündoğan managed it perfectly well enough at the other end. It's intense provocation and a fan throws a lighter at them. You can never condone this, but you can certainly understand why someone would do it.

The replays of the penalty incident show that the ball clips Grealish's fingernails. Any change in speed or direction is indiscernible and for sure nowhere near enough to have denied them any kind of scoring opportunity – the ball was heading into an area populated solely by City players. For many observers, that's enough to brand the decision ludicrous, but it isn't. It's the rules around the definition of what constitutes handball that are ludicrous.

We've had some similarly contentious decisions go both for and against us this season, but at least the ones that went our way came when we were on top and looking likely to score. This one has catapulted them from a position of being a goal behind and completely outplayed to one of parity, a status they've done absolutely nothing to deserve. It's that double sense of injustice that really hurts, and it isn't the first time.

One of my worst nights in recent years, at least in terms of watching football, was when United beat PSG in the Champions League on away goals via an added-time penalty. As United pressed forward with seconds remaining, needing a goal to turn defeat into victory, Diogo Dalot launched a shot from just outside the area with a trajectory which would have sent it at least ten yards over the bar. The ball struck a PSG defender and went out for a corner. Lucky bastards, I thought – Dalot's dreadful, desperate effort deserved to see the PSG keeper take his time over the goal kick, launch it downfield and hear the final whistle. Instead, they've now got a corner to defend.

But it's so much luckier than that. Amid genuine disbelief from the hosts, the ref goes across to the screen and is persuaded to point to the spot. How can it be right when a shot destined for row 23 strikes the arm of a bloke who's not even looking at it and ends up deciding the game? Where's the justice in that? Rashford scores, United go through and Solskjær is proclaimed as the Messiah, the man who'll lead them back to their former glories. Nothing can go wrong now Ole's behind the wheel.

But not much goes right either. After a couple of years of achieving nothing of note, Solskjær was sacked and United were back to the shambolic mess we've come to know and love. In came the cleverest man in football, the legendary Ralf Rangnick, as United fans were kidded into thinking they'd unearthed a footballing mastermind while everyone else wondered if this guy's so good, why's no one ever heard of him? The answer rapidly became apparent, Rangnick presiding over a comically incompetent spell as United lurched from embarrassment to embarrassment. The new United were becoming the old City. And their fans plenty bitter enough to make it a convincing impersonation.

But now it's Ten Hag's turn to lead them back to the glory days. We all hope and expect that we're looking at another false dawn but with this kind of luck, who can say? They go in at half-time level, their fans dancing in jubilation while we're all utterly downcast. Up in the stands, Ferguson gives a sickly smile, not out of pleasure at United's performance, more a reaction to a mini 'football – bloody hell!' moment.

At half-time, the BBC turn to Peter Schmeichel, who technically has a foot in both camps – eight trophy-laden years at United, one swansong season at City when he was almost 40 years of age. Despite that, he still ranks among City's greatest goalkeepers of all time and watching him play for us, in Maine Road's final season, made you wonder just how many fewer trophies United would have won without him. Schmeichel never makes any attempt to hide where his loyalties lie but he's surprisingly honest in his half-time appraisal. 'I'm sat here thinking it's 1-1. How's it 1-1? Manchester City are totally dominating everything.'

Despite the setback, we carry on controlling the game as the second half begins. Five minutes in and Fred commits a foul on De Bruyne which makes you wonder whether this referee is ever going to issue a card. The offence was near the corner flag but De Bruyne would have been left with a clear run and the chance to set up a scoring opportunity. Instead we get a free kick akin to a corner, but we make it count. Kev pulls his cross back to the edge of the area – an increasingly common ploy in recent games, frequently looking for Foden – but on this occasion his target is Captain İlkay. Gundo strikes the ball on the full, but it's nowhere near as clean a connection as his 12-second special. No matter; the ball bounces twice as it skips towards the net, somehow avoiding the massed ranks of United defenders who've also served to leave De Gea partially unsighted. The keeper reacts too late, and though he gets his fingertips to the ball it's not enough to prevent it entering the net.

My celebrations are muted if almost non-existent, as they so often have been in the VAR regime. From my angle I sense that a City player may have been offside as Gundo struck the ball. Could he have been in De Gea's eyeline? No one has appealed but, as we've seen so painfully so many times before, that means nothing. But after the celebrations on the pitch subside, United kick off and only then do I let out a yell of delight. Replays show that the City player who'd caught my eye was Rúben Dias, and he was well onside. I'd never make a linesman.

What a player Gündoğan is! His last three domestic starts have seen him produce two goals in each, all of them vital, and this is the first one to have had a touch of good fortune about it. As we seek to extend our lead, Grealish squares the ball to Haaland whose low shot on the turn, first-time as ever, is kept out by a smart save by De Gea. Gündoğan pounces on the rebound to clip the ball home, but the instant and correctly raised offside flag cuts short any thought of joining the Stan Mortensen club. And keeps United in contention.

The introduction of Garnacho gives their attack a bit more pep, and when he cuts inside his attempt to curl the ball just inside Ortega's far post is only just wide. Still, it's City who remain the more threatening and a marauding run from Haaland almost sees him carve his way through the centre of the United defence. Then, as time runs down, Wout Weghorst, the bluntest of blunt instruments, lurches on to the pitch and they resort to getting it in the mixer. In stoppage time, a knockdown sees Ortega dive at McTominay's feet and the ball loops up and bounces off the top of the crossbar. Weghorst looks favourite to get to the rebound but with a prodigious leap Rodri manages to prevent him getting a clean header and the ball goes just over the top. It's a narrow squeak but it's the last scare we have to endure before the joyous sound of the final whistle.

As anticipated, United fans prove supremely efficient at emptying their half of the stadium – and though there's plenty of mockery, I'd have been out of there like a shot had the result gone against us – allowing us to celebrate in time-honoured fashion. 'We'll be running round Wembley with the Cup' is a chant long consigned to the archives –

what's the point when half of it's empty? We later read that one of their number had the bright idea of turning up with a shirt number 97, bearing the words 'Not Enough' where the player's name normally goes. For pissed-up tribal hordes to indulge in such chanting is bad enough, but for someone to make a considered decision to get such a shirt printed and think it's a good idea really does beggar belief. Rather than having his mates collapse in hysterics at such a witty gesture, he finds himself arrested and hopefully banged up for a good while. Ideally with plenty of Scousers.

* * *

Gündoğan takes the man of the match award and makes all the headlines, as usually happens when your goals have won the cup, but for most of us today's star performer has been John Stones. What a revelation he's been. His new role is frequently described as hybrid but because we usually enjoy most of the possession, he's more akin to a holding midfielder, but one with licence to roam.

He's not always been a first choice during his seven years at the club but for sure he's a player that Pep has loved from day one, a player the manager knew he could help mould into something special. When Stones made one of several costly errors in his first season, Pep laid into his critics in memorable fashion at the post-match press conference. 'John Stones has more personality than all of us here in this room. More balls than everyone here, guys. Under this pressure from all of you, people criticise him for this huge amount of mistakes, he still comes out and wants to play. It's not easy to play central defender with this manager.'

But Stones managed to do it with increasing authority, retaining his composure on the ball while cutting down on the errors. Still there were the odd difficult periods, and when City signed both Rúben Dias and Nathan Aké in the summer of 2020, it looked like he might be on the way out. But although offers to join either Arsenal or Chelsea were there, he decided to stay and fight for his place. Stones said, 'I started being super critical of myself and looking at what I could do better on the football pitch. I looked into every detail, down to what food I was eating, my training, what extras I could do. I would go home and work there, even late at night, or straight after the training. I wanted to find these small margins, and put them all together to break where I was at. I wanted to prove to myself that I belonged here. It was a big learning curve for me and made me who I am today.'

And what he is today is an absolute Rolls-Royce of a player, who's evidently surprised even himself with the ease with which he's slotted into this new role. And he's become a real fan favourite, chants of 'Johnny, Johnny Stones' ringing out repeatedly before, during and after games home and away. He's as one of our most loved, most valuable players, and his best years are still ahead of him. Those big balls have served him well.

* * *

Ten Hag's interview after the game is disappointing in the extreme, with barely a word of congratulation towards City. His suggestion that United had fought their way back into the game is laughable. Having delivered a threat rating of absolutely zero, they were gifted a penalty from a situation of no danger whatsoever. We're informed that the handball rule will be changed next year so that penalties will no longer be awarded for such incidents. Thanks a lot. It's the second time this year that United have scored goals against us – via VAR – which in any other season would not have been allowed. At least this one didn't cost us.

Ten Hag goes on to claim that United could have equalised near the end, which is certainly true, but he at least stops short of saying that they would have deserved to do so. If it wasn't quite a '2-1 massacre' it was certainly a match in which the closeness of the scoreline doesn't fully reflect the run of play. But that doesn't matter. We've won the cup and almost immediately the talk turns to the next week's Champions League Final – and the Treble. This is something of a shame. Derby wins are to be savoured and celebrated, a derby win in a cup final even more so, and yet by some it's being treated as a mere stepping stone towards a greater objective. Not by the players though. They'll be allowed to let their hair down and party tonight – celebrating success is a crucial part of this club's culture. It should never be taken for granted.

And Jack certainly doesn't need any excuse to celebrate, although he's still at a loss to comprehend why the penalty was given against him. 'I could understand it if I was looking at the ball, but I had my back to it.' And he was well aware that his would have been the name in the frame had the incident led to a United win, as he smiled and said, 'Gundo saved me!' Asked whether he'll be going out to party even though there's a date with destiny next week, he surprises nobody. 'Course I am, you don't win the FA Cup every week!' while emphasising that he'll be back in for recovery tomorrow.

And I'll need to do a bit of recovering myself. If you measure the magnitude of a win by the consequences if you'd have lost then this one is right up there. The endless gloating, the 'we stopped the Treble' delight wouldn't have abated even if we do go on to win the Champions League. But we'll worry about that next week. For now, it's time to celebrate a victory summed up beautifully by Oliver Brown in *The Telegraph*. 'City were not at their best in this final, and yet the superiority in quality over United was so glaring that it left Sir Alex Ferguson looking as if he had just chewed a wasp.' These days it seems to be his only expression.

30

10 June 2023, Champions League Final: City 1 Inter Milan 0

'Tonight, the Manchester rain will taste like champagne'

SO IT'S off to Istanbul. I've been once before and it's far from my favourite city, but you can't not be there. We have various friends that we're hoping to meet, but in this monstrous sprawling mess of a place, if you're not based in the same area then it's pretty much impossible. But at least young Tom has taken my advice, shelled out for a ticket, and booked himself a hotel nearby, so we're a gang of three on this, the season's final adventure.

This is a massive event for the host city. All the bars and restaurants are decked out in either City or Inter colours – sometimes both – and the streets are flooded with staff trying to lure punters in with the promise of wonderful local cuisine at bargain prices. They're lying. The cuisine is not wonderful. I end up going for simple dishes where you'd hope nothing could go wrong, but I'm evidently the victim of a linguistic misunderstanding. When I said I wanted my steak rare, they must have thought I said cremated. They should have served it in an urn.

There are pre-match interviews galore with players and managers, and Pep sounds a note of caution to those who make City the overwhelming favourites, which is pretty much everybody. 'A final against an Italian team is not the best gift. It's not a coincidence that Italian teams are there in all three European finals. And others in semi-finals as well. I play there, and I know the mentality of Italian teams in finals.' Overlay the fact that Champions League finals are such nervy affairs in any event, frequently settled by a single goal, and no one should be taking anything for granted. Inter, meanwhile, claim to be undaunted about the task in front of them. 'You are scared of assassins and murderers, not football players,' says defender Alessandro Bastoni. 'There's no fear, just the right level of tension. More than anything, there is happiness.'

There are plenty of nice snippets emerging from the City player interviews, notably Kevin De Bruyne. When asked about Erling Haaland and whether it was 'love at first sight when you met in the summer' he paused, smiled, and replied, 'No, I'm happy with my wife.' But he did acknowledge that the two of them had a special relationship on the pitch. 'Sometimes you have a feeling with a player where you understand what he wants and he understands what I can do,' Kev added, going on to reiterate what Pep has said many times before. 'One of the best attributes I've discovered working with him is that he can miss one chance and he is not getting depressed, not sad. He is always thinking positive, next one. He knows he will have the chance and he will be there. This is an incredible attribute.'

Kev is also asked about his apparent spat with Pep during the Madrid game. 'It's not a problem for me. It's never personal. In the end, everyone always wants to get the best out of each other. So much is written about that incident, but here we never talk about it again. Those are moments between competitive people. I don't see a problem with that. Everyone just wants to win.' And this is a game that Erling wants to win as much as anyone, as he gives an insight as to the special burden on his shoulders. 'Of course I feel pressure. I would lie if I said I didn't. They won the Premier League without me, they won every trophy apart from this without me. So I'm here to try to do a thing that the club has never done before. It would mean everything.'

For City fans, the journey to the stadium is excruciating, typically taking some two and a half hours in ageing shuttle buses which significantly predate the incorporation of air-conditioning. And that's after you've stood in the – literally – mile-long queue to get on board in the first place. Holding the final in a stadium 25km outside the city centre with no public transport available (other than a metro which we're advised not to use) and the most congested road network in Europe isn't a recipe for a stress-free journey. But we get there, manage a couple of beers in the fan park, and make our way inside the ground hours ahead of kick-off. Only the most patient can avail themselves of further refreshments, as the paucity of outlets generates queues which snake around the concourses for several hundred yards. This is a venue patently not fit for purpose, and there can be only one reason for its selection. And they wonder why we boo the anthem.

The stadium does at least possess big screens at either end, and we see images of the two team coaches on their way to the ground. Hopefully the drivers have got a bit of local knowledge or else the kick-off will have to be delayed. Aboard the City coach, third keeper Scott Carson, once of Liverpool, tries to calm nerves by referencing 'The Miracle Of Istanbul'. 'Don't worry, boys. Every time I come to Istanbul, I leave with a Champions League trophy,' he says.

The team news comes through. For a few years now, the joke doing the rounds among journalists has been that one day Pep will overthink his XI so much that he'll pick the right team by accident and win the Champions League. But there's no overthinking this time. There's just one small surprise, with Nathan Aké coming in for Kyle Walker. I assume that Kyle hasn't recovered from the knock he took last week, until I see that he's listed on the subs' bench. In reality, it's Akanji rather than Aké who'll take his place on the right, presumably a factor being that Inter don't have wingers of the same pace that Real can boast.

The pre-match entertainment constitutes a dazzling array of lights with various performers that those of us over 30 years of age have never heard of. Is anybody actually taking it in? There's a splendidly choreographed army of dancers, together with a woman on a podium gyrating in the fashion of Britney Spears 20 years ago, and that was bad enough at the time. Have we not moved on since then? All we want is for the match to start. As the teams come out, most of the City fans get their vocal chords ready for the traditional jeering of the Champions League anthem, but UEFA have a cunning plan to thwart this show of disrespect. Instead of the usual pompous overblown assault on the ears that normally accompanies the entrance of the teams, they've got some bloke with a piano to play it live. This understated rendition is so different that hardly anyone recognises it, and it has the desired effect, at least as far as UEFA are concerned.

Milan's tactics are obvious from the kick-off; indeed, they were obvious long before it. Five at the back, a combative midfield three snapping into tackles in midfield and two up front. They let us have the ball up to 40 yards out but the space is compressed and it's not going to be pretty.

We fashion a couple of early half-chances, firstly when some typical Bernardo trickery ends with an angled curler which just passes Onana's far post with the keeper clearly fearing the worst. And then, even though there's so little space, De Bruyne slides in Haaland whose pace over five yards allows him to escape from Bastoni. It's a decent chance, but a slightly heavy touch takes the ball just too wide for him to wrap his foot around it, and he can't find the angle to get his shot across Onana. Inter, meanwhile don't create anything of note, but there are still plenty of nerves in City's defence, with the second of two misplaced Ederson clearances going straight to Barella, who thankfully miscues his attempt to chip the ball over the stranded keeper.

But the big headline from the first half is an injury to Kevin De Bruyne. After just 35 minutes his hamstring, which has needed careful management over the last two months, finally gives way at the worst possible moment. Kev trudges off, visibly trying to keep his emotions in check, and although there are a couple of consoling pats there isn't really much anyone can say. It's a serious blow for the team, and absolutely cruel on De Bruyne, who fell victim to Rüdiger's brutality two years ago and had to leave that final prematurely as well. But it does give Phil Foden the chance to make his mark, stepping into the central midfield role which he's surely destined to fill for many years to come. He's looked in great nick over the last few weeks and would start for every other team in Europe, so let's not feel too sorry for ourselves.

The second half sees us continue to dominate possession while only occasionally achieving phases of fluency. Nerves and tension are still evident, with a quite abnormal series of misplaced passes causing Pep to cut an increasingly anguished figure. He's edging ever closer to Roberto

Mancini's Basil Fawlty impression so realistically delivered in the period leading up to the Agüero Moment. We have to stay patient and remind ourselves that we're still level. Don't do anything stupid at the back and eventually the chance we need will come.

But then, out of the blue, we do something stupid. When Bernardo passes the ball back down the right, Akanji assumes that Ederson will come to collect it. But he doesn't. Lautaro Martínez pounces and cuts inside. Lukaku, by now on as sub for Džeko, is making a run for a cut-back but Lautaro instead tries to beat Ederson from the angle, and the keeper spreads himself to make a crucial block. Dias was sprinting across to cover Lukaku but whether he'd have got there in time to intercept we'll never know. It's a horrible moment, Pep sinking to his knees as the drama unfolds. A chilling reminder that one little mistake is all it takes to destroy a dream.

And one little moment of inspiration is all it takes to fulfil one. When Foden receives the ball inside the Inter area, he's forced backwards and it looks as though he's going nowhere. But as soon as the angle's there, he switches the ball across to Manu Akanji, some 40 yards out but, for the first time all evening, with some serious space in front of him. Akanji moves forward and threads the ball between two Inter defenders – one of whom, Dimarco, crucially slips in his efforts to intercept – and the line has been broken. Bernardo races on to it and both Haaland and Gundo have a chance of a tap in if he can slide the ball into the right channel. Meanwhile, Foden sprints from the edge of the area and brings three defenders back with him, meaning that as Bernardo attempts his cross, the edge of the six-yard box is seriously congested. Bernardo's ball strikes the nearest defender and deflects away from its target but, as Foden appeals half-heartedly for handball, his run, and Dimarco's inability to prise himself from the ground, has created a chasm. The central area between the six and 18-yard lines is completely vacant.

The ball travels towards the edge of the area, and Rodri runs on to it unopposed. As he shapes to strike for goal I'm instantaneously transported back to one of our most iconic moments: the 2011 FA Cup Final, when Yaya strode on to a similarly deflected pass to thrash the ball home and end a 35-year trophy drought. Now, Rodri is the man charged with replicating the feat and putting us en route to an even bigger landmark. There's no one I'd more like the ball to have fallen to. He's had the time to set himself, has a clear sight of goal and is such a clean striker of the ball. All he has to do is put out of his head the magnitude of the moment, the glare of every one of the 71,000 fans inside the stadium and the 450 million watching worldwide, the fact that this could – literally – see him immortalised, fulfilling at last the quest for European glory which was first frustrated in this very city 55 years ago, while cementing the team's status as one of the greatest in football history. Pressure, what pressure?

I really think he's going to score and as soon as he strikes the ball it's never in doubt. The ball passes behind two static Inter defenders, each of whose only chance of stopping it would be to stick out an arm to concede a penalty and a red card. Neither of them move a muscle as the ball passes them both as well as the similarly motionless Onana. The net bulges and the celebrations begin. It's a moment that every City fan present will never forget.

We've been nervy and way below our best, but we're where we need to be. Inter's game plan had to a large extent worked but now they'll have to commit more bodies to attack. They do so immediately and within a couple of minutes they're almost rewarded when Dimarco's header loops over Ederson, who strains desperately but can't quite reach the ball. It rebounds off the bar, straight back to Dimarco, who heads it goalwards, only to see it strike Lukaku and rebound to safety. It's a desperately close shave which underlines the fact that we've got more than 20 minutes of increasingly unbearable tension to come. Unless.

The unless moment arrives almost immediately. Foden takes possession 30 yards out and executes a bewitching sleight of foot which will require several slow-motion replays to understand exactly how he did it. The ball sits perfectly in his stride and he sprints into the area to bear down on Onana. I think he's going to score. Phil elects to go across the keeper rather than opening up his body to slide it by him. He's highly adept at giving opponents the eye, but here he telegraphs his intentions and Onana makes a comfortable save. Pep gesticulates in anguish as the chance to breathe more easily dissipates instantly. It's the last one there'll be until the final whistle blows.

At the other end, Lukaku is making an obvious and most unwelcome difference. He's a beast, one of the very few in world football capable of bullying Dias, and he's actually doing it, holding up the ball, bringing others into play and scaring the life out of 20,000 Blues at the other end of the stadium. He's had plenty of ridicule for the chances he's missed against us over the years but he's putting the fear of God into us right now. He runs at Dias inside the area before drilling a shot straight at Ederson. We're all trying not to look at the clock at the top-right of the big stadium screen – a watched pot never boils – but it's impossible not to do so.

Just two minutes remain when Inter manipulate the ball back to Brozović, with space and time to measure a telling cross. The ball curls beyond the far post where Gosens outjumps Bernardo to head across the face of goal. There, absolutely central, five yards out and unmarked, is Lukaku. He can't miss. Can he?

His header isn't the cleanest, but from that distance anything even a yard wide of Ederson will end up in the net. Instead, it's almost straight at the keeper, and Eddie gets his knee in the way, deflecting the ball into the ground and directly at Rúben Dias, who has no time to take evasive action. It looks like a certain own goal – where else can the ball go – but Dias contorts his neck violently as he tries to direct it to safety. By a matter of inches, he succeeds, as the ball just passes the far post to go out for a corner. It's a miraculous escape, with Inzaghi on his knees on the pitch, where he'd trespassed in premature celebration.

Undeterred, Lukaku again runs at Dias to give himself a sniff of a chance, but screws his shot well wide. The Blues jeer, but it's not with ridicule – it's 100 per cent relief. The added-time board sentences us to five more minutes, and the bloke behind me counts the time down, very loudly, in 30-second intervals. Inter's approach is less than subtle – repeatedly playing the ball back for Onana to launch forward – but it's effective, as it seems like they're winning every aerial duel. The last of the prescribed 30 seconds approaches its conclusion and Inter win a corner. For them it's now or never. Up comes Onana and we all know the score. Head this one away and we're there.

Dimarco whips in a flat, pacy in-swinger towards the near post. It's an excellent delivery and is met perfectly by Gosens, whose glancing header speeds towards the net. I've seen this film before. It's another of those flashbacks. Ben Watson in the 2013 FA Cup Final, whose late near-post header from a corner flashed beyond Joe Hart to win the cup for Wigan. But this time Ederson flings up an arm to deflect the ball away, and Bernardo ensures its passage out of play. Just as we wonder whether that's the end of the ordeal, the City players leap in ecstasy. None of us have heard the referee's whistle, but we don't need to.

There are the scenes everywhere on the pitch, all the players in tears of joy or despair. It's basically the same as it always is, but it feels different when it's your team. Pep is calm initially, but is soon on the pitch hugging anyone he can get his hands on, more emotional by the second. He has a tearful embrace with Kevin De Bruyne, captured by the cameras. 'We did it! We did it! We did it! Seven years of fighting! We did it, Kev! Now we have it!' his voice cracking with emotion. It takes a few minutes of exultation for me to remember that we haven't just won the Champions League – we've won the Treble. This is historic. It's why we came to Istanbul.

After a few more minutes it's time to get our hands on the trophy, and at least the presentation doesn't take place against the backdrop of a half-empty stadium, as the vast majority of Inter fans stay around to watch before filing out to leave us to our celebrations. And there are some seriously emotional scenes, blending the almost disbelieving ecstasy of our newest recruits – Haaland, Akanji and Lewis having won the Treble in their first season, and Álvarez the ultimate quadruple, for God's sake – with the relief of team-mates who've spent years in search of this trophy, and endured so many bitter disappointments along the way. And that certainly also goes for the vast majority of City fans in the stadium.

One man who'd have wanted to be among us was Noel Gallagher, but he'd evidently failed to factor in the season's extended schedule when organising his US tour, instead having to watch the game in a San Diego bar. His post-match reaction was recorded for posterity, and found him at his most poetic. 'There have been so many nights when these fans have travelled home from Europe battered, bruised, beaten and conquered. But not this time. Because tonight the Manchester rain will taste like champagne.' Definitely words worth setting to music.

* * *

Rodri is named man of the match, with the fact that he scored the goal doubtless a major factor. And his all-round game, as ever, was really strong. But the man whose contribution is freshest in our minds is Ederson.

Earlier in the season, there was apparently some sort of clamour on fans' forums – as if those opinions would ever influence Pep – for Ederson to be dropped, that he wasn't as good as before, that he wasn't just not making many saves but that his feted distribution had become less accurate and less effective. When he first arrived, no one in England had seen this type of goalkeeper before. His pinged 40-yard passes and press-beating balls threaded through small gaps were something different, and opponents naturally began to take steps to close off his passing lines, just as they would for a 'normal' defender. So of course it's become more difficult for him to be so effective, so constructive and, unlike the rest of our players, the scope for him to show versatility and change position isn't quite there (however much you suspect he'd enjoy it). But he remains an essential part of our build-up play, with his close control and calmness under pressure an enormous asset. If his passing stats are less impressive than when he first arrived, that simply reflects the fact that his targets are both fewer and smaller.

Those ill-judged dives at strikers' feet to concede penalties are something we haven't seen in a while, and we have to accept that taking on the role of 'sweeper keeper' involves an element of risk, and that the odd misjudgement as to when to come hurtling out of his area is inevitable. But these aberrations really are just occasional nowadays – off the top of my head, I can only recall the Leipzig home game this season.

As for shot-stopping, I've never seen what the fuss is about. Now and then you think, in the words of the TV pundits, that 'he might have done better with that' but when was the last time he properly chucked one in in the manner of a De Gea or an Alisson or a Pickford or a Lloris? And when it came to this season's Champions League, his interventions in the big games were as important as anyone's. From repelling the Sané salvo in the first leg against Munich to those vital late saves from Benzema and Tchouaméni to preserve parity in Madrid, his was a vital contribution in our reaching Istanbul. And when we got there, his performance was perhaps the most important of all.

The saves from Martínez and Lukaku were crucial, but it was the night's final action, when he leapt to keep out Gosens' glancing header, that will cement his place in folklore when the tale of this match is recounted in years to come. Overlooked on TV because it was followed immediately by the final whistle and accompanying general hysteria, this was a phenomenal effort, with the ball travelling at a searing pace above a mass of players and requiring nimble footwork as well as the sharpest of reflexes to get a hand to it. Had that gone in, it's hard to imagine Inter not having gone on to win the trophy.

* * *

After the various TV channels have had their minutes with the players, it's Pep's turn. How's he feeling? 'Tired, calm, satisfied of course.' A shake of the head and a wry smile. 'This fucking trophy, it's so difficult to win it.' The apology to the viewers is hardly necessary as it's well beyond the watershed. In Turkey it's already tomorrow. Pep is asked what the difference is between this and the 2021 defeat to Chelsea, and he says that we're defending better in the box, 'Now we enjoy defending.'

With four centre-halves we have defenders who love to defend, who relish the duels, and that's what's allowed the John Stones tactical shift to be so effective. But, however you choose to dress it up, the main reason we won was that Inter missed two sitters. Our number, at last, came up and Pep's honest about it. 'You have to be lucky. This competition is a coin toss.' It's basically what he'd been saying year after year but now, after he at last called correctly, at least some of the media might give some credence to the line he'd consistently adopted. 'It was written in the stars.'

Players are being grabbed for interviews on and around the pitch, and most of it is stuff we've heard a thousand times before. But what else can you reasonably expect them to say? There is, however, one striking exception. Kyle Walker talks about how gutted he was not to make the starting line-up and reveals that, just before the teams made their way out, he put aside his personal disappointment to make a short speech to his team-mates. 'This has always been my dream. My dream is in your hands. Go out and make my dream come true.'

It's a fabulous example of the mentality which Pep has instilled in this squad. After being told he'd miss out on what could prove to be the most prestigious and celebrated game in our history, to be able put this aside to help motivate his colleagues was a proper demonstration of team spirit. He might be prone to acts of embarrassing dickheadery away from football, but this showed a level of maturity above and beyond. And no one could begrudge him his belated appearance as a substitute, ensuring that he was on the pitch at the moment those dreams really did come true.

So, as the party on the pitch, then behind the goal close to the City fans, comes to a close, it's time for us to head back into Istanbul. It's a similarly protracted journey, and when we finally arrive, beyond 3am, there are a few Blues milling around in the bars having a quiet drink. Certainly in our part of this hideous mess of a city, there's no party atmosphere, let alone one befitting our team's momentous achievement. UEFA's lamentable choice of venue has drained us of the energy. Doesn't mean we aren't happy, but the wild, exuberant celebrations you'd imagine would take place on a night like this aren't in evidence at all. We expected to expend a lot of emotional energy today, but the physically draining ordeal of getting to and from the stadium has simply wiped us out.

So it's a quiet drink, bed at 4am, and a nap rather than a sleep before setting off to the airport. We're way too early, having left the sort of margin you clearly need in a place like this, only to find that our taxi driver is evidently auditioning for the role of the Turkish Ayrton Senna. He and we just about avoid meeting the same fate as the Brazilian legend, only for our flight to then be delayed by 90 minutes.

And if it hadn't been for those 90 minutes late on Saturday night, this would have been the worst, least enjoyable, most frustrating weekend break I'd ever taken in my life. But give it a week or so and I'll be looking back on it with nothing but affection. For the rest of my days.

Aftermath

WHILE CITY had been hoovering up the trophies, Erling Haaland had been doing the same thing with the individual awards. He took the Football Writers' Association's Footballer of the Year award with an extraordinary 82 per cent of the vote, and also became the first player ever to be named the Premier League's Player of the Year and Young Player of the Year in the same season. He then went on to win the PFA Player of the Year Award. Has any player ever made a greater impact in their first season in English football?

Haaland's record of one goal in the final eight games of the season did suggest a drop-off in form, and he certainly missed a few where you'd have expected him to score. But he was also the victim of some inspired goalkeeping and there was a definite sense that his game was evolving. His greater involvement in the build-up play progressed significantly as the season went on, and the increased focus on this aspect of his play, the extra energy expended in participating more fully, may have taken a little away from the precision of his finishing. Or maybe that's just a coincidence.

In the latter part of the season we were certainly playing the ball up to him more frequently, allowing him get into that lay it back, spin and sprint routine. Four times since the beginning of March he scored goals based on this template;

none at all in the 33 he netted beforehand. This is definitely not a coincidence.

What's for sure is that when all the facets of his play come together, and his development under Pep continues, he might well make a useful striker. And the fear factor he brings to opposition defenders, the space he creates for others, has so often been an important factor in City making vital breakthroughs. Defenders are affected not just by what he actually does, but also what he might do.

He was supposedly bought to make the difference in tight games, and yet his only winning goals in the Premier League came from penalties at home to Fulham and at Palace. The only time he struck an open-play winner was against Dortmund in the Champions League. He scored plenty of goals that put us ahead, but then frequently added to his tally to put us out of reach. Haaland didn't so much make the difference in tight games, he more made sure that games weren't tight at all, hence the number of occasions he was substituted well before the end. Making the difference in tight games usually requires you to stay on the pitch for the whole match. Getting the job done early is far less stressful and affords vital rest.

His 36 top-flight goals for City were the most in one season since Southampton's Ron Davies hit 37 in 1966/67, while his 52 goals in all competitions was the highest tally since Dixie Dean's 63 for Everton in 1927/28. His four Premier League hat-tricks were as many as all other players combined and he was the first top-flight player to record six hat-tricks in all competitions since United's Denis Law in 1963/64. Of his 52 goals, all but six were scored with a single touch. This ratio might be more common for strikers who score a high proportion of headers, but it's remarkable for a player who, despite his height, does most of his damage on the ground. And none of this appears to have gone to his head.

Rodri: 'Erling is very simple, he's still only 22, he's just a kid. He's so humble and wants to learn and listen, he has the hunger to improve, and when you have this many good things can happen.'

Gundo: 'Honestly, I didn't know what to expect when he came here. You see the goals and all the attention that he was getting at Dortmund, and you wonder if he's going to fit with the group. But when I got to know him, I was so surprised how someone could be that talented and still have the will to be even better every single day. He's never satisfied. I feel like there are no limits for him. Messi and Ronaldo are the only comparison for the level he could reach.'

And that desire to improve was illustrated perfectly in Haaland's interview with CBS Sports after the Champions League Final, where he turned the tables and asked Thierry Henry a question. 'Where do you think I can improve? Give me one advice.' Thierry told him that when he spins after having his back to goal, he should sometimes make the subsequent runs to his right as well as to his left. At this point fellow pundit Peter Schmeichel pleaded, 'Stop it! No more advice!'

Second-season syndrome is something generally associated with promoted sides, who often struggle once teams have sussed out how they play. After such a spectacular start to his City career, could a similar thing affect Haaland? Maybe it will, but against this is not just his unquenchable desire to keep on getting better but also the fact that City players generally take a full season to fully embrace what Pep wants them to do, and develop accordingly. Oh dear.

But it looks as though he'll need to up his strike rate significantly if he wants to break Sergio's goalscoring record.

According to his dad Alfie, 'Erling wants to test out his capabilities in every league. Then he can stay in every league for three to four years maximum.' Perhaps he'll stay until Pep leaves. Perhaps, like Pep, he'll enjoy being here so much that he stays longer than originally planned. Whatever, let's enjoy him while we've got him. We may never see his like again.

* * *

A couple of weeks after lifting that most elusive of trophies, İlkay Gündoğan ended speculation about his future by confirming that he would, after all be moving to Barcelona. Our club captains do have a habit of bowing out with impeccable timing. In 2019, Vincent Kompany announced his exit straight after we'd completed the domestic treble, a feat which was and remains unique. And now İlkay's followed suit, choosing to move on at a point where things can't really get any better. It's an emotional departure for an immensely popular and influential player, and one who'll be sorely missed.

Gundo took the decision to pen an open letter to City fans, and it contained some interesting insights. 'For me, the Champions League has been a bit of an obsession for the last ten years. Well, not a *bit*, actually. It's been an obsession, truly. When my Dortmund team lost the final to Bayern in 2013, I was crushed. There is no feeling like losing a final. It seriously haunted me for ten years. Every decision I made in my career since then has been about lifting that trophy. That's why I came to City.' And he emphasised how the emotions on finally lifting the trophy were if not greater then certainly different for the players who'd tried again and again and again, as opposed to the more recent recruits. 'The struggle is always worth something. The years of failure is what made the victory so overwhelming, and so sweet.'

He referred to Kyle Walker's dressing-room speech and the impact it had on his colleagues, and saved some words for Jack. 'I just want to say that Jack Grealish is so misunderstood by some of the media. He is one of the nicest guys I've met in football. He's so much fun to be around and so humble and pure. He worked so hard to get to another level this season, and he was fantastic for us.'

Indeed, as the season progressed the real nature of Jack's personality came out more and more, and there's a straightforward unguarded innocence about his interviews which is really endearing, illustrated again by his words in Istanbul. 'Today I was awful. To win the treble with this group, it's so special,' he said. 'I'm a family person, I love football so much, it's what I worked for all my life. You think back to all the people who have helped me all the way. It's emotional. Pep's a genius, I told him, "I want to thank you, buying me for all that money." Last year I was playing crap, but he stuck with me.'

So maybe he's nothing like what so many of us imagined, at least when he's sober. And perhaps that ill-judged Almirón insult was just a function of his natural unguardedness – the sort of thing players might joke about in the dressing room but which most others would keep to themselves in public. Humble pie time. I was convinced he wouldn't make it.

The players' celebrations instantly became the stuff of legend, almost as much as the achievements which generated them. Inevitably at the epicentre was Grealish, dragging half the squad off for an overnight jaunt to Ibiza before they returned to a Manchester under deluge for the official parade on Monday afternoon. There, incongruously sporting a high-visibility jacket – the sort of thing you'd do after a particularly brutal stag do, it was surprising he didn't have a traffic cone on his head as well – Jack claimed not to have slept for 36 hours. It certainly looked like it, though he was far from alone. Stories of excess crept out in the media, but really, if you can't celebrate an achievement like this then what's the point? There were a few admonishing voices, but I don't think any of them were City fans. When you've delivered like this, you've earned the right to celebrate however you like.

Legacy

SO WHERE does this side sit in the pantheon of great teams down the ages? Obviously there will be those who immediately point to the Premier League charges hanging over us and that this should preclude such discussions. But let's assume for now that none of them go on to be proven, just as we assume that none of the other great sides of previous eras perpetrated any shady deals, provided under-the-counter inducements to enable them to sign important players, attempted to bribe officials or opposition players or cheated on the pitch.

There'll also be those who'll say that we have an unfair advantage because of our ownership and the money we've spent. That we should be winning everything, given the advantage that affords us. But this is becoming an increasingly invalid argument. Of course we've bought success, but so has every other successful side. And plenty have bought failure, some of them spending more than we have in the process.

These days the metric most used in assessing who the big spenders are is net spend. It's probably as good as any, but by carefully choosing the period of assessment you can often manipulate the figures to support the point you're trying to make. But a five-year period gives a decent representation, and based on this, at the time of writing, City aren't even in the top ten net spenders. Extend the period to ten years and we're second in the list. But who's above us? United. Rather than bleating about the Glazers, maybe their fans' venom should be directed at those responsible for their club's decisions in the transfer market. Their top six buys comprise Pogba, Antony, Sancho, Maguire, Di María and Lukaku. Half a billion quid's worth of abysmal underachievement. Maybe Antony will come good, but the rest?

For sure we've made mistakes, but our strike rate with big-money transfers is better than anyone's, and our recruitment process and principles are well defined. Most recently with Declan Rice, we've had a ceiling for each potential target beyond which we're not prepared to go and more often than not it's served us well. And it turns out that we've dodged a good few bullets, notably when the player in question has instead gone to United.

And talking of them, as soon as we'd completed the Treble, comparisons with United's 1999 team abounded, with conclusions naturally shaped by whose side you're on. I'd hate anyone to think I was even slightly biased, so it's time to dust down the magic hat of impartiality.

Looking at the bare statistics, United won the 1999 title with just 79 points. There has been no lower winning total since. It hardly suggests that they were a dominant force that season, and but for Arsenal's surprise defeat at Elland Road in their penultimate game United would have finished second. City's total of 89 points may – or may not – have been even greater had it not been for the fact that the final two fixtures were dead rubbers, but the ruthless finishing streak of 12 straight wins, incorporating an annihilation of our nearest rivals, on the face of it cements our place as a more dominant team in our era than United were in theirs.

It could of course equally be argued United's low winning total reflects a more even league of greater competitiveness, that it was more difficult to put together winning runs. The two previous seasons each saw even lower winning totals, which does support this assertion, but the figures immediately before and after this phase were significantly higher, several of them achieved by United themselves. A more realistic conclusion is that United's 1999 side wasn't even their best of that era, rather just the one that got lucky. And that's definitely supported when you look at their two cup campaigns.

In the FA Cup, United had some real 'our name's on the cup' moments, scoring twice in the last two minutes to overturn Liverpool's 1-0 lead in the fourth round. And then in the semi-final replay, they were spared when Dennis Bergkamp missed an injury-time penalty which would have sent Arsenal to Wembley. Instead the game went to extra time and Ryan Giggs scored a goal that hardly anyone has ever talked about since, putting them through to see off a feeble Newcastle side in the final.

City, meanwhile, saw off both Arsenal and Chelsea in the early rounds and reached the final without even conceding a goal. They would have retained that record had it not been for the absurd handball law, and although there was a narrow squeak at the end, the victory in the final, against a side with more motivation to stop us than any cup final opponent in history, was universally regarded as being comprehensive and well deserved.

In the Champions League, United came through a very difficult group, including Barça and Bayern, and also had to mount a stirring comeback to defeat Juventus in the semi-final. But their final victory was one of those scarcely credible travesties of justice that make football the great game it is, outplayed by a far superior Bayern side only for two late goals to deliver an unforgettable memory, albeit an excruciating one for so many of us.

City's group was less demanding, but then to beat comprehensively the two teams regarded as Europe's finest outside the Premier League was an outstanding achievement. We saved our luck for the final, a match that certainly could have gone the other way. But it was still an evenly balanced affair, nothing like the United-Bayern game.

Overall, it's undeniable that City's degree of dominance over our opposition in our Treble season was far greater – and our reliance on luck far lower – than United's was in theirs. That supports a case for City being the stronger side, but does it make our achievement greater than theirs?

No one can dispute that United's Treble will always be the more memorable, partly because it was the first time it had been achieved but also because of the moments of sheer drama it contained, not least in the final against Bayern. And that's fair enough. After all, City's Agüero Moment Premier League victory is so much more memorable than those where we cruised to the title. Our Pep-era champion teams were all clearly superior to the Roberto Mancini vintage, but it's Mancini's team which created the most indelible memory.

So maybe the conclusion should be that the City Treble winners are the better team but that United's achievement in winning it is the greater. Winning the Treble when you're clearly the best team has to be easier than doing it when there are opponents at least as good and arguably better than you.

As the season reached its climax, Wayne Rooney at least met this conclusion halfway. 'If they win the Champions League and the title, much as it pains me, I think you'd have to put City up there with United's 1999 Treble winners as the best Premier League team of all time. Our 2008 United team were also a great side but the way City dominate opponents and make it look so easy, so often – while constantly fighting on all fronts – is beyond what we did.'

The last word goes to Jason Burt of the *Daily Telegraph*: 'In winning the Treble in 1999 Manchester United were an incredible team but it felt a bit more "seat-of-the-pants". City just dominate in a way that the sport has never witnessed before in this country. For all their swashbuckling brilliance, that United side never produced the utterly stunning, aesthetically perfect football that City played in destroying the European champions Real in the first half in Manchester. It was arguably the most complete performance ever from an English team in European competition and City have been close to that level several times.'

* * *

Another frequent point of comparison is the managers: Ferguson and Guardiola, both legends who'll be remembered forever. Ferguson's trophy haul at Old Trafford is astonishing and unlikely to be matched by anyone at a single club. But in terms of their broader levels of influence on football in England, indeed Europe, there's no comparison.

As far as the English game is concerned, it's not an exaggeration to say that there was football before Pep and football after Pep. Most obviously, we now take it for granted that teams will play out from the back, and that the process will start with the goalkeeper, making ability with the feet a far more important attribute than ever before.

When Pep replaced Joe Hart with Claudio Bravo, Bravo's first game, in the Manchester derby, saw him produce a haphazard display in which he was lucky not to be sent off and came close to costing City a win their performance had otherwise richly deserved. Pep defended Bravo to the hilt afterwards, praising his courage to carry on trying to play the way he wanted even though he didn't appear to be doing it very well.

There's a thin line between genius and madness and at this stage plenty of City fans wondered which side of it Pep was on. Surely by far the greatest attribute of a goalkeeper, the only one that really mattered, was an ability to keep the ball out of the net. Yet look at the way almost all of the teams play now, and an essential part of their build up process is the goalkeeper. When United signed André Onana recently, descriptions of his qualities *began* with his ability to play passes out from the back. If they'd signed him ten years ago, this characteristic wouldn't even have got a mention.

Pep's use of Lewis and Stones in the hybrid role this season was admired, absorbed and then increasingly copied by Premier League managers. It is inevitable that the new season will see this taken on across the league – and also that Pep will be looking for further tactical nuances to keep opponents guessing. Seldom if ever has a manager been so committed to exploring the art of the possible.

City's core attacking strategy through the Pep era has embraced orthodox wingers, inverted wingers, false nines and now the big man up front. Admittedly not any old big man but a change still requiring a different approach, structure and tactics from the rest of the team. The core principles of dominating possession, looking to create overloads, pressing to recover the ball as quickly as possible, have never changed, but there are so many variations within that, and Pep's already shown himself to be flexible enough to mix things up in order to utilise Haaland more effectively.

He's often accused of having it easy, managing the biggest teams with the biggest budgets and the best players. And, of course, there's truth in that, but his real skill has been how he's developed those talents. How many of them play in positions they never previously imagined possible? John Stones is far from the first. And how many of them say the way they think about football has been transformed by working with Pep? Thierry Henry, already a magnificent, elite player when he arrived at Barcelona, gave an insight into how Pep gets into players' heads. 'I thought I was kind of OK, but I arrived there and he deprogrammed then reprogrammed me to a certain way of understanding the game.' And there's a sense that this is already happening with Haaland, that in Pep's eyes a 52-goals-a-season striker is still very much a work in progress.

In terms of dressing room culture, Pep's approach is to create a harmonious group with as little friction between players as possible, with everyone buying into the team ethic and supporting each other. Ferguson's was to get a bunch of ferocious competitors to give their all and not give a damn whether they got on with each other or not. And this was where he truly excelled. To get such a collection of difficult, combustible, egocentric and ostensibly often thoroughly unpleasant characters such as Keane, Neville, Stam, Schmeichel and Cole to gel into a consistently successful team was an incredible achievement. Cole and Sheringham supposedly never even spoke to each other during their time together at Old Trafford. This was taking United's 'no one likes us, we don't care' mantra to a new dimension. Could Pep have managed those characters so successfully? Could anyone?

But while Ferguson obviously excelled in the area of man-management and motivation and for all the success he brought to United, his broader influence on the game has been negligible, other than making systematic intimidation of officials a depressingly common feature of modern football. If it works, people will copy it, and it certainly worked for Ferguson and his team. You wouldn't call it the greatest legacy. Andy D'Urso still has sleepless nights.

On the face of it, their managerial styles could hardly be more different but, although they express it in different ways, they're both ferociously competitive, demanding that their players give everything for the cause. Pep's football may be more aesthetically pleasing, more technical, but it's underpinned by the requirement to win the duels, to compete for everything. His 'happy flowers' outburst demonstrated perfectly what he expects. Desire, passion, fire. There's an iron fist inside that velvet glove. And for his broader impact on the game and ongoing influence, his innovation and ingenuity, the beauty of the football his teams produce and, of course, his enormous success, Pep will surely always be remembered as the ultimate football manager. And he still has power to add.

* * *

So, finally, having chosen Guardiola as its manager, what would a composite side of the two treble winning squads, the best of the best, look like? It's tough to compare players from different generations but fortunately there are some key factors we can use in order to reach an objective verdict.

Goalkeeper: Peter Schmeichel was indisputably the better shot-stopper, and also had superior command of his penalty area. But playing for a Pep team requires a keeper good with his feet, something Schmeichel was seldom required to demonstrate at United. Could he have done it? All we have to go on are his hapless lumbering performances on *Strictly Come Dancing*, which demonstrated a terrifying lack of co-ordination in his footwork. His dismal foxtrot proved to be the final straw for the judges, and similar clumsiness with the ball at his feet would inevitably result in a multitude of disastrous and costly blunders. This makes Ederson by far the safer choice.

Defenders: Kyle Walker's physicality and pace make him an obvious selection at right-back, and in any event Gary Neville is excluded purely on the grounds that he's bloody 'orrible. Based on comments he made in his autobiography, Jaap Stam would have little argument with Neville's exclusion, but the very fact that the Dutchman resorted to making a few quid by slagging off his former colleagues shows a blatant disregard for team spirit. Consequently, the inspirational Rúben Dias has to be preferred. John Stones's class, versatility and impressive credentials in the testicular department naturally make him a shoo-in over Ronnie Johnsen, but it's a close call at left-back, with Denis Irwin's reliability pitched against Nathan Aké's versatility across the back line. However, Aké's teetotaller status gives him an invaluable advantage, allowing him to act as designated driver for the multitude of celebratory events which this team would surely enjoy.

Holding midfielder: Roy Keane's inspiring leadership and competitive nature would be a huge asset for any team, but his predilection for acts of extreme, mindless and brutal violence means that under modern refereeing codes he'd rarely even make it to half-time. So it's a clear nod for Rodri.

Attacking midfield/wingers: Kevin De Bruyne versus David Beckham is self-evidently a mismatch, with Kev not only able to bend it like Beckham but capable of passes that this most overrated of all United players could never even contemplate. With De Bruyne's selection, Paul Scholes is automatically excluded under the admittedly little-known 'One Club, One Ginger' rule, allowing Bernardo to slot in, while Phil Foden's skill, invention, adaptability and ability to catch carp allows him to edge out Ryan Giggs, who would at least relish the opportunity to spend more time with his family. Battle of the party animals Jack Grealish and Dwight Yorke would most fairly be decided on alcoholic consumption capacity grounds, and Jack's performance during his post-Istanbul three-day bender, one day per trophy won, just gets him over the line. And certainly over the limit.

Striker: Andy 'call me Andrew' Cole isn't even close to a match for Erling Haaland. But then who is?

And so the composite City/United Treble winners side would look something like this.

Ederson

Walker Stones Dias Aké

Rodri

De Bruyne Bernardo

Foden Haaland Grealish

Manager: Guardiola

It's a beautifully balanced side, fully representative of the very best that Manchester football has ever had to offer. Can you imagine what it would be like to see it in action? What a treat that would be ...